KU-266-050

WHERE TO START AND WHAT TO ASK

WHERE TO START AND WHAT TO ASK

An Assessment Handbook

SUSAN LUKAS

W. W. Norton & Company
New York • London

For information about permission to reproduce selections from this book,
write to Permissions, W. W. Norton & Company, Inc.,
500 Fifth Avenue, New York, NY 10110

For information about special discounts for bulk purchases, please contact
W. W. Norton Special Sales at specialsales@wwnorton.com or 800-233-4830

Manufacturing by Courier Westford
Book design by Justine Burkat Trubey
Production manager: Leeann Graham

Library of Congress has cataloged another edition as follows

Lukas, Susan Ries.
Where to start and what to ask : an assessment handbook / Susan Lukas.
p. cm.
"A Norton professional book."
ISBN 0-393-70148-4 (cloth) - ISBN 0-393-70152-2 (paper).
1. Interviewing in psychiatry. 2. Interviewing in mental health.
I. Title.
[DNLM: 1. Interview, Psychological-methods.
2. Psychological Tests-methods. WM 141 L954w]
RC480.7.L85 1993
158'.39-dc20
DNLM/DLC
for Library of Congress 92-49934 CIP

ISBN: 978-0-393-70784-7

W. W. Norton & Company, Inc.
500 Fifth Avenue, New York, N.Y. 10110
www.wwnorton.com

W. W. Norton & Company Ltd.
Castle House, 75/76 Wells Street, London W1T 3QT

1 2 3 4 5 6 7 8 9 0

For Kit, Megan and Gaby
who make anything seem possible

CONTENTS

ACKNOWLEDGMENTS

I am grateful to many people for their help with this book. To my three student readers: Diana Manchester, Tracy Vandenbergh, and Deirdre Maloney. To Maurice Elias, of the Rutgers University Department of Psychology, for his kindness to a stranger. To Susan Donner, Director of Field Placement at Smith College School of Social Work for her thoughtful and astute comments. To Judith Rosenberger of the Hunter College School of Social Work for her enthusiasm and encouragement and for allowing me the benefit of her students' observations. To my publisher and editor, Susan Barrows Munro of W.W. Norton and Company, for her guidance, her vision, and most of all, her regard for writers and the written word.

Professionally, I have the good fortune to be surrounded by caring, dedicated clinicians. At the Jewish Board of Family and Children's Services I am especially grateful for Patricia Nitzburg's insight, her wit, her forbearance, and her steady hand on the tiller, and for Annaclare Van Dalen's goodness, her brilliance, her profound understanding of human emotion, and her belief in me when I need it most. These two women and Emily Shachter—whose wisdom and style I treasure—personify the professional standards to which I continue to aspire.

Finally, I wish to acknowledge my abiding debt to Professor Charles Guzzetta of the Hunter College School of Social Work who, from my first day in academia to the moment of this writing, remains an inspiration. Without his intellectual rigor, his dedication to teaching and learning, his spirit of generosity, and his good old-fashioned work ethic, this book might never have been written.

THE HOW AND WHY OF
THIS BOOK: AN INTRODUCTION

Within a few weeks after I began my field placement as a social work student in an MSW program, I asked my supervisor what he thought was the most essential feature of being a good beginning clinician. "First of all," he said, "you gotta know your customer." Glib as that phrase may sound, it embodies the highest principles of sound practice and useful intervention.

Further, by helping me to focus on where to begin, it helped me not to feel anxious all the time, which is the way I felt on the day I asked my supervisor that question, and which is the way I quickly discovered most of my fellow students also felt. To be sure, some of that anxiety is unavoidable; some of it is quite useful in making sure that we don't overstep our knowledge or authority and that we turn to our supervisors for guidance.

The degree to which we are able to present those supervisors with factual information about our clients,* as well as with our impressions, is the degree to which they can help us assemble that information into a coherent understanding of the clients' problems and needs. The purpose of this book is nothing more nor less than to help you accomplish that information-gathering in a concise, thorough, and systematic way—which should also help diminish some of *your* anxiety.

---

* Since I am trained as a social worker, I will refer throughout this book to those being served as *clients*. Depending on the setting in which you train, or your profession, you may be more accustomed to referring to them as *patients*.

The book is not going to provide you with all the "answers." It *will* provide you with numerous questions and describe the situations in which they might be asked. That does not mean that you are going to direct all of them to the client. Some you are going to ask of yourself after an interview. Some you are going to discuss with your supervisor. Some you may never have occasion to ask. The idea of this book is simply to have them available to you when and if you need them.

The time at which you are likely to need these questions most is what's known in clinical parlance as the *assessment phase*. The purpose of the assessment phase is to help you and your supervisor make an accurate diagnosis, on the basis of which you can then formulate a conscientious treatment plan. In some agencies and institutions the assessment phase is embodied in the protocol of the agency; that is, you will be expected, during the first series of interviews to producefrequently in writing* – some statement of the nature of the presenting problem, a background history of the client, a sense of the underlying pathology (if any), and some preliminary judgment as to whether or not there is a match between the kinds of services your agency provides and the prospective client's needs.

No doubt this last paragraph has raised far more questions in your mind than it has answered, first and foremost of which is: Am I going to be expected to do this on my own? And the answer is no. You will get a great deal of help, most of all from your supervisor. In addition, much of the content of your courses will be aimed specifically at assisting you in making these judgments.

Unfortunately, little of this may occur before you actually start interviewing clients. And even after you start getting supervision, it is almost impossible to get as much help as you feel you need. Why?

First, because supervisors are busy people. They have their own case loads and frequently have other administrative responsibilities, as well as supervision of other students and staff, so they have to remember a great deal about many cases. In

---

* This written document may be referred to in your agency as an *assessment, or a comprehensive assessment,* or a *diagnostic assessment,* or any of a number of other names. Again, since I am trained as a social worker, it will be referred to here as a *biopsychosocial assessment.*

addition, your time with your supervisor will be limited by your own schedule, so it is crucial for you to provide as much information as possible in the limited time you have together.

Second, unless yours is an agency that permits you to audiotape your interviews (and this practice raises some thorny ethical and clinical issues), it is unlikely that your supervisor will ever know *exactly* what happened in an interview. You may write a process recording which recounts some, or maybe even most, of what was said, maybe even how you felt or what the client was doing when he* said it. But, no matter how hard you try to remember, some of it will be lost. In addition, it is entirely possible that your supervisor will never actually see that person (there are exceptions, e.g., if the case is transferred to you from your supervisor, or if you work in an institutional setting and clients are known to the staff), so your supervisor must rely heavily on the information you provide.

So, for a while you are going to feel a great deal of anxiety when you start an interview. You are going to be worrying about what you're supposed to do or say next, at the same time as you are trying to listen, look, think, pay attention to what you are feeling, and make some sense out of all of it. In short, you are going to have to learn to tolerate the feeling of *not knowing*.

If that sounds abstract or philosophical, be assured that it is not. You are immediately going to be confronted in your interviews with clients who are in pain, who frequently have experienced unthinkable deprivations in their life, and who want-or appear to want-answers. And you are going to feel an intense desire to act, to do, to be reassuring and to say something that will instantaneously make them feel better. So why not do it?

---

* Hereafter, the client's gender will be "she" in odd-numbered chapters and "he" in even-numbered chapters. In all chapters the therapist will be referred to as "she." These designations do not always reflect statistical correctness, logical correctness, or political correctness. They are simply intended to make the book easier to read. Obviously, you will substitute the appropriate pronoun when your judgment and experience indicate you should do so.

In those chapters that refer to "parents," it is hoped that your common sense will again prevail, and you will remind yourself that a child is not always parented by his or her *biological* parents, nor by two people of opposite sexes, nor even necessarily by *two* parents at all.

The answer to that question is quite straightforward. In most cases, you don't know the person to whom you are listening. You may have read a file on that person. You may have been given some information about his background. But you have no idea what makes him tick. You may have some hunches, but you don't *know* what his life is like, what comforts him, what frightens him. Therefore, you have no way of judging how your client will use the information or advice you might be inclined to offer. In the best case, your helpful comments might be ignored or give false reassurance in a situation that needs to be better understood. In the worst case they may be dangerous to him or those around him. The purpose in saying this is not to scare you; it is to move you in the direction of thinking about each client as unique, of recognizing that the human psyche is subtle, complex, and to be regarded with the utmost respect.

Having said all this, having posed these dilemmas and restrictions on the help you can obtain from others, we come to why this book has been written. It is intended to help you resist the impulse to formulate premature hypotheses, to help you withstand some of the feelings of helplessness and frustration that come from waiting and not knowing, and to give you some guidelines for discovering who the person sitting before you really is. It is going to give you some direction for conducting different types of interviews, as well as some standardized tools for making an assessment. It will point you in the direction of what you need to know and how to discover it and give you some clues as to where to look next. All this is intended to help you produce a document that you, your supervisor, and the treatment team can use to answer one crucial question: How do you respond to this particular client in a way that is truly therapeutic?

Before we begin the assessment phase, a few more words about the book and its orientation. First, it is written as if you were working in a community mental health clinic serving a culturally and ethnically diverse population of men, women, and children. Therefore, you may find at times that you need to adapt the material to your clinical setting and the unique circumstances and characteristics of your clients.

Second, though my own training is psychodynamically oriented and there may be unintentional indications of that in the text from time to time, the book is not meant to reflect any particular theoretical perspective on how to do treatment. Every professional school and every discipline is different. Individual professors have their own beliefs as to what works and what doesn't when it comes to treatment modalities (e.g., group, individual counseling, family intervention) and you probably have your own inclinations as well. A school or its faculty may reflect the dominance of one theoretician or another (e.g., classical Freudian thinking, self psychology, object relations, behaviorism, or a combination of these and many others). However, regardless of your orientation or your school's, responsible and thorough assessment is crucial.

If you are experiencing doubts about your own ability to tolerate not knowing long enough to do a thorough assessment, two final pieces of information might be useful.

This one may *seem* obvious but it is easily forgotten when you are face-to-face with your first client: Remember that the person who is sitting opposite you has probably had these problems for a very long time. Even if the person is a child or you are responding to a recent trauma or you are working with a family, the intrapsychic and interpersonal characteristics have been there awhile. Change is going to take time. You are neither a miracle worker nor a magician, and what you are embarking on is a mutual task, one in which you and the client (or clients) are going to work together to understand what parts of the present approach to the problem are useful and what parts aren't. However, implicit in that mutual effort is your understanding that the client has developed, or was endowed with, some strengths for coping with those problems. It is vitally important that in doing your assessment you discover those strengths and help the client to recognize and build on them. If you doubt the existence of those strengths when you are confronted with your first client, remember that—no matter how disturbed he may seem—he is talking, working, playing, eating, and somehow going on with his life. Also remember that, even if that person seems unable to function, there is some small part of him that wishes to be healthy or he wouldn't be alive.

Lastly, if you aren't already, at some point you are going to feel overwhelmed with questions about your right to be practicing and learning on your clients. At such moments it is important to remember that you probably have a smaller case load than the regular workers in the agency and, therefore, more time to devote to each of your clients. Furthermore, your caring, your dedication, and your interest will go a long way toward building a relationship with a client, and that relationship is the cornerstone on which every client's experience of being helped rests.

WHERE TO START AND WHAT TO ASK

one

How to Conduct the First Interview with an Adult

We are now ready to begin addressing the first interview. The book will describe many such "first interviews," aimed at different client configurations and various types of issues; however, regardless of the configuration, your goals in a first interview are always the same:

- First, to allow the client to tell you her own story in her own words. You may have voluminous documents that you have read before your first interview; however, it is still crucial that you hear—or elicit—the client's understanding of why she is there and what *she* thinks the problem is. This does not in any way imply that you necessarily accept, or even agree with, the client's interpretation or definition. It simply means that you want to hear it from her.
- Second, to let the client know that you understand what she believes, even if it is her belief that she does not need to be there. This involves listening carefully to what the client is telling you and acknowledging it by something as simple as saying, "Are you saying that you are having difficulty in your relationship with your husband?" Or, "Maybe you're saying that you would really rather not be here."

The client's realization that you are an interested listener and that you are making an effort to understand her is the essential first step in engaging any client in treatment. If you disagree with the client's perception of the problem, this is not the time to say so. Depending on the nature of the treatment (e.g., family therapy), you may restate the family's perception of the problem using a different framework, but that will be taken up in the chapter on the first family interview. For now, just remember that the overriding purpose of any first interview is to listen and to let the client know that you are trying to understand.

With that premise in mind let us go on to the first interview with an adult. This chapter might have been called "The First Interview with the *Self-Referred* Adult," because what it focuses on is the client who comes because she herself recognizes a need to explore the possibility of therapy. The operative words are "explore the possibility." What that means is that the person feels she needs help with a problem. It *doesn't* mean she necessarily knows how to define the problem she is struggling with; it *doesn't* mean she necessarily knows what therapy is or whether it can help her with the problem; and it certainly *doesn't* mean that she necessarily wants you to be her therapist. Helping a client with all those things is part of your job. But before you can begin—in fact, before that person walks through the door—you must prepare yourself.

In many agencies part of your preparation will be reading some documentation on the client. That may be nothing more than a two-line summary of the problem the client has reported and a telephone number you can call to set up an appointment. On the other hand, if the case is being transferred to you, it may mean a huge file that includes a medical history, a psychiatric evaluation, a mental status exam, a biopsychosocial assessment by a previous clinician (or clinicians), that clinician's progress notes, a report of psychological testing, a diagnostic code, and many other types of information.

Whether it is one page or fifty, though, your response ought to be the same: What don't I know that I need to know? Start making some written notes for yourself, beginning with those questions that you need to have answered before you call the client back to arrange an appointment. For instance, you may want further clarification of her current problem, if possible, so you can be sure she is coming to the right place. You may want

---

WHAT TO ASK YOUR SUPERVISOR
BEFORE YOUR FIRST INTERVIEW

1. **Any questions raised by your reading of the client's case record.**
2. **Whom to include in the first interview.**
3. **How long the session should last.**
4. **How often you should see the client.**
5. **How to introduce yourself.**
6. **When and how to record the contents of the first interview.**

---

to find out if anyone told her there is a fee charged. Or, if the case appears to involve more than one person, you may want to inquire about who should be included in the first interview. You should raise those questions with your supervisor or with the person who had the initial phone contact.

Then, if you have voluminous records to read, start by asking yourself what's missing. If there are no medical records, why not? (You will find more on the importance of medical information in Chapter Three.) If that person was seen at another agency, were the records requested and have they arrived? If the person is taking medication, what kind, how much, and who's giving it to her? Start taking notes about the basic facts: age, ethnicity, who's in the family, presenting problem, I.Q. scores, diagnosis, etc. Begin to build a profile on that person in your mind, ask questions, do your homework—and then add a healthy dose of skepticism to everything you've found out.

Why? Because your job is to find out who that person *really* is, and the information in a file is only as useful and accurate as the competence and insight of the people reporting it. For example, I.Q. scores can easily be affected by the client's mental state when the testing was done. Diagnoses often vary depending on the clinician, the purpose of the diagnosis, and the circumstances under which the client was seen. Intake information may have been taken in English, while the client's first language is Spanish, or Chinese, or Farsi. The medical information may include only an emergency room visit at a local hospital and not the records of the client's primary care physician. In addition, what you are reading may reflect another clinician's inexperience or prejudice or hostility toward a client. Since you don't know what factors are at work, it is important to be aware of the inconsistencies in the record and to wonder about them.

If you are supposed to telephone the client, remember that your relationship starts when she answers the phone. Be professional and concerned but remember that the purpose of the call is not to do therapy over the telephone but to arrange a mutually convenient time when you can meet face-to-face. The client may be anxious; however, do not assume that you know what that anxiety is about. Also remember that asking for help is not an easy thing to do.

So, now you've arranged the first interview. What next? If you are fortunate enough to have your own office, take a look around and ask yourself how you would feel coming there. If your client is likely to bring a child, is there anything for the child to play with so you can talk to the parent? If the client is in a wheelchair, can she get through the door or do you need to meet in some other office? If the client has trouble speaking English, would it be reassuring to have someone there to translate, or would it be insulting? And lastly, do you have pictures of your current partner or your children on your desk or other personal memorabilia around? If so, it's probably a good idea to ask your supervisor's opinion about whether or not to put them away, since they have to do with who you are and not with who the client is, and you have no idea what meaning the client will attribute to them or how she will see you once she has seen them.

Now you have prepared yourself for your first interview. The next question is: How will you remember what the client tells you? There are many schools of thought:

- Never take notes, just listen carefully.
- Always have pad and pencil handy to jot down a phrase or note that will jog your memory.
- Audiotape.
- Don't audiotape.

Your answer will probably rest someplace between what your agency feels is appropriate and your own sense of how anxious or distracted you're going to feel. Even if your agency feels that note-taking, in general, is a bad idea—because it seems too impersonal or will divert your attention from the client—the exception is almost certainly going to be the first interview. You need to get some basic data and you need to get it accurately. One option is to inform the client that recording information accurately is the purpose of your note-taking and ask her if she feels comfortable with your doing that. Most clients will say "yes"; however, if one doesn't you will simply be confronted with the need to cultivate an essential habit: that is, making *some* notes after every interview. The word *some* is emphasized because you will not always have time to write down everything. If you make it a practice to note five or six key phrases or observations, you will probably be able to reconstruct much of what happened.

Now you are ready to greet the client. This moment is important. Although it may vary slightly depending on how many people are involved and the circumstances under which you are seeing the client, there are a few basic principles intended to transmit courtesy, interest, and a clear message that this is a professional rather than a social relationship.

If at all possible, you should always go out and meet the client rather than having her sent to your office by a receptionist. Opinions vary on whether you should introduce yourself more or less formally, e.g., "I'm Ms. Lukas" versus "I'm Susan Lukas" versus "I'm Susan." They also vary on the issue of whether or not to shake hands with clients. Depending on her clinical outlook and the circumstances under which a client is coming for therapy, your supervisor may feel that any physical contact might transmit a misleading or potentially threatening notion about therapy. Therefore, all these questions should be discussed before the first interview.

Having greeted the client, and while leading the way to your office, you should remember that the interview has already started. Listen very carefully to what the client is saying and make a mental note of your overall first impression. When you have ushered her in, pay attention to how the client reacts to your office. What does she say? Where and how does she choose to sit? (If possible, you should arrange seating so the client can sit facing you at a distance that permits her to speak in a normal voice, but is far enough away so that she does not feel you could reach out and touch her. If the client comes from a culture in which reaching out and touching another person's arm is a sign of friendship or interest, then she can move the chair closer to you if *she* chooses to.) Does she wait for you to suggest that she sit down? Does she sit on the edge of the chair? Does she seem disorganized?

Try to help the client to feel more comfortable. Show her where she can hang her coat if she wants to. Suggest that she might feel more comfortable in another seat. But remember: If the client chooses not to do any of these things, do not urge her to. The goal is to "start where the client is," rather than expecting her to do it your way. You are concerned with *her* feeling of what is comfortable, not yours.

Once the client is seated, if she starts talking, let her. And pay very close attention. Often, the first things the client tells you are the most significant. If she doesn't start talking, you might want to introduce yourself again, this time adding to the introduction the fact that you are an intern (or extern, or student, or whatever phrase your school or agency prefers). If you know you will be staying in the agency for only a limited time, ask your supervisor or your school what the policy is concerning when to inform your client of that fact. Some feel it is best to let the client know at the beginning that you are a student and will be leaving the agency on a given date. Others feel it is better to proceed as if you were just another member of the staff and to wait until the client is engaged to tell her about your departure. You will have to find a position on this issue that is comfortable for you, but it is best to clarify it before you start interviewing clients.

Some clients may pursue this issue. They may want to know more about your credentials, or they may tell you they were "expecting to see a doctor." You may need to explain something about how the agency works and who comprises the staff. Or this may lead to a discussion of the client's previous experience with therapy. It is generally best, however, not to get into an extended discussion about who *you* are. For instance, some clients may express the feeling that you are too young (or too old) to understand their problem, while others may feel that you cannot know what it is like to be a parent if you've never had a child. Usually, these concerns will fade over the next few interviews, as you demonstrate your interest and professionalism. In the meantime, unless you feel, or have been told, that there is a compelling reason to do so, the less you reveal about yourself the better. This can often be accomplished by explaining that the purpose of your meeting together is to help the client understand the difficulties she is struggling with. If this seems withholding, remember that the focus of concern should remain on the *client's* needs and how best to meet them.

One way to impart this feeling is to help the client start talking about what brought her here. This can be a straightforward question. Or, if you know something about the client's situation from the intake information, you might want to guide her by saying something like, "I know your husband died two months ago. Can you tell me more about that?" Remember, the purpose of the interview, no matter how much you know, is to get the client to tell you her own story in her own words.

And while she is talking, the most important tasks you have are to listen and not put words (or feelings) into the client's mouth. What that means is that the client may describe to you a situation that would make *you* feel angry, or frightened, or helpless. However, that's not necessarily what the *client* feels or can accept that she feels. Therefore, you need to respond with language that is as emotionally neutral as possible. Stay away from loaded words like "furious" or "incompetent" or "I would have felt. . . ." Also, avoid clinical jargon like "depressed" or "anxious" or "guilty." Let the client tell you what she is experiencing by simply listening or saying something like, "That sounds like it was very difficult for you," or, "I can see this is very painful for you." Let the client define what difficult means or what it is that is painful for her.

This sounds as though you are supposed to remain mute while the client tells her story. That is not the case. It is probably more useful to think of yourself as arriving in a new country and trying to understand what the customs are. If the client comes from a different race or religion or social circumstance, there will be both cultural and personal values that are different. Your job is simply to be aware of that and not to judge her experience by your own. In addition, you will be exploring the unique terrain of this person's life. You should feel free to ask questions about her experience. For instance, "Mary is your sister-in-law?" or "Did you move a lot?" or "It sounds like things changed a lot after your mother died." And most importantly, it is okay to say, "I don't understand." Remember, the client will appreciate your interest in her, and asking her to help clarify who or what or when or how is a way of demonstrating your interest.

The question to avoid, however, is "Why?" For instance, "Why did your father do that?" or "Why did you feel that way?" or "Why can't you tell your brother that?" These questions call for an understanding of motivation and for a response that suggests insight about the client's own behavior or the behavior of others. They are also implicitly asking the client to articulate feelings. She may do that spontaneously, but it is best not to ask for feelings yet. There are a number of reasons for this.

First, and most obvious, the client may not know the answer. She may never even have thought about the question before. In that case, you run the risk of making her feel inadequate, which is certainly not the way you want to make her feel. The second possibility is that she may know an answer but the answer she knows is a source of conflict for her, in which case she's going to avoid telling you but come away with the impression that therapy is going to force her to tell you things she is not yet prepared to talk about.

The third possibility is that she may tell you far more than she meant to tell you. It may feel at the time like you are having a wonderful interview in which the client is being "open" and "able to get in touch with a lot of her feelings." The risk in such an event, however, is that you may never see her again. She may leave feeling she has "spilled her guts," frightened or humiliated that she has told her inner thoughts to a stranger. Remember,

---

REMEMBER

• **Ask who, what, when, where and how. Don't ask why.**

she has a right—and you have an obligation—to protect her from a sense of premature intrusion into her private feelings, particularly since you have not assessed what effect such revelations will have on her functioning.

The sum total of all this, then, is that you want to ask only about facts and information the client can provide without having to probe her feelings or motivations. After all, if she were clear about her feelings, she probably wouldn't be coming for help with a problem in the first place. Furthermore, asking "why" can lead you into making premature judgments about the client's problem, since you will be fighting the desire for explanations and conclusions.

So, what information do you want to gather during this first interview? Foremost is her description of why she is here *now* as opposed to six months ago or six years ago (this is known in clinical parlance as the "presenting problem"). You want the basic data if you don't have them: name, age, marital status, occupation; with whom she lives and where; any previous experiences of therapy; and perhaps some preliminary information about her family of origin. You also want to get some sense of her support system: Does she have friends? Do her relatives live nearby? Does she have a good working relationship with colleagues at her job? Many of these answers will emerge spontaneously. If they don't, ask for them.

Toward the end of the session, you want to leave yourself enough time to ask the client if she has any questions. In addition, you want to ask whether she would like to come back again and talk further. You might help her make that decision by pointing out what you are seeing, e.g., that she seems to be struggling with her feelings about her father's death or that it is sometimes difficult to know the right thing to do when you are having trouble with your child.

The goal here is to try and arrive at a mutual definition, in language that seems right to the client, of what the presenting problem is. Under the best circumstances the client will say something like, "That's exactly the way I would have said it." If you do not reach a mutual definition, however, that is not a reason to despair, since you are new at this. It is perfectly alright to suggest that the client return again so you can further explore and clarify what it is she would like your help with.

If the client does want to come back you need to arrange a time to meet again; in addition, if your agency requires it, you need her to sign some kind of permission to provide services. You may also need to discuss how fees are paid, insurance coverage, and other documents that may need to be filled out.

The client may also raise the question of confidentiality: Who will know about what is discussed between the two of you? This issue will be discussed in a number of different contexts later in the book, but it is important for now to realize that there are some exceptions in practice to the notion that client confidentiality will be upheld at all costs. For instance, information is usually shared in agencies where there is a team approach to treatment decisions. Also, in most settings where students train, there are seminars or other learning situations in which group discussions of cases occur. More importantly, in instances involving certain risks of danger to the client or others, there are exceptions in the law to your right to keep information confidential.

You should discuss these issues with your supervisor in advance. You need to find out what exceptions prevail and get some basic guidelines so that you will be prepared and comfortable in talking with your clients about how things work in your

---

CONFIDENTIALITY

1. **Find out if, and under what circumstances, you are required by law *not* to maintain confidentiality.**

2. **Except in those circumstances, always get *written* consent from your client to share information about her with other agencies.**

3. **When you get a telephone call about a client, always remember that even the fact that she is attending therapy is confidential information that you can release only with the client's permission.**

4. **When you present cases outside your agency, always change clients' names and disguise their life circumstances sufficiently to protect confidentiality.**

agency. Usually, after noting the exceptions, you should be able to reassure the client that no information about her will leave the agency without her written consent.

Once you have established the parameters of confidentiality, you must get in the habit of observing them even when it *seems* unnecessary. You must learn to disguise the names of clients when talking about them, unless it is absolutely essential to use their real names. When you discuss cases with people outside your agency—and many would question if this is a sound practice at all—you should give as little information as possible and disguise what you do give. When you talk to colleagues at school, remember that the world really is a small one; when you talk to colleagues at work, it is best to do so in the privacy of your own office, not where other clients might overhear the conversation.

So, you and your new client have agreed to meet again next week. Perhaps, depending on how your agency works, you have told her that you will meet for 45 minutes once each week. Or perhaps you have agreed that you will discuss with the treatment team what approach would be most useful and that you will report those findings to her at the next session. It is often helpful to give the client a card noting the date and time of your next meeting. (You may not want to do this for all clients. It's a judgment you'll have to make at the time.) However, it is best to do this without asking the client if she needs it, since you may embarrass her. As you will discover, clients cancel or miss appointments for many reasons, but not knowing the date or time should not be one of them.

You are now ready to end the session and usher your new client out. You rise and walk to the door; then, as your client is about to leave, she says, "Well, I guess next week I'll have to tell you about the time my father tried to kill himself." This is known as the "door-knob syndrome": that is, the client waits to tell you some piece of information that is terribly important or frightening or embarrassing until there is no time to discuss it further. The general rule is to say something like, "That sounds like something we should discuss further. Let's begin with that next week," and not to allow the session to be prolonged. This is a way of letting the client know that she has a limited amount of time in which to talk with you each week and that it will be more useful if she brings up disturbing issues when you have time to explore them together. The notable exception to this general principle, however, is if the client says something like, "Next week I guess I'll have to tell you about the time *I* tried to kill myself." This issue will be covered more thoroughly in Chapter Nine; for now simply remember that you *never* let a client leave your office if you have any sense that she may do herself, or someone else, harm.

In brief, that is the first interview with an adult client. In the next chapter we will look more carefully at the three areas on which you are going to be concentrating your attention while you are meeting with the client: looking, listening, and feeling.

two

LOOKING, LISTENING, AND FEELING: THE MENTAL STATUS EXAM

Now that your first interview is over, you must leave yourself enough time in your schedule to think about it and to make notes, first and foremost, of what you have observed. Again, there is an operative phrase here: "what you have observed." We will talk further on in this chapter about the importance of your own feelings while the client is in your office, but the place to begin organizing your thinking about a client is with the observable.

This process of noting the observable in some systematic way is referred to as the mental status exam (MSE). It is different from the biopsychosocial assessment, although the two frequently appear together in the case record. The biopsychosocial assessment is based mostly on facts about the client's life and a description of the problem which *the client* has provided you during a series of interviews. The mental status exam is essentially *your* observations. It is used in different ways in different clinical settings, but those differences have more to do with the time at which one formulates one's findings than they do with content.

For example, the results of a mental status examination might be used to hospitalize a patient after an initial interview, or they might not be formulated until the sixth session, when the biopsychosocial assessment is being prepared; in either case, however, the *contents* of the mental status exam and the *order* in which you note your observations are always the same. In fact, the mental status exam is probably the most widely used assessment tool among mental health professionals.

As you will quickly discover in reading this chapter, "widely used" is not the same as "easily used." In fact, the mental status exam is filled with phrases and concepts that take awhile to learn. The first time you read them they will almost certainly seem both abstract and overwhelming. Even if you do succeed in getting a loose handle on them before your first interview, you will probably still need to go back and re-read them after that interview and several others before gaining any feeling that they are a routine part of your assessment of a client.

The question then becomes: Why even *think* about the mental status exam now rather than later-much less try and write one-especially since you are unsure of yourself and the agency might not even require it for a while? The best answer is that the mental status exam is an extremely useful tool for assessing a client *over time.* That is, conceptualizing your initial mental status exam as a snapshot taken at the first interview, to be followed periodically by new snapshots, is going to help you understand what part of the client's initial presentation has to do with the stress of the moment and what part reflects his basic personality.

In addition, using the mental status exam in this way offers an ongoing opportunity to formalize answers for yourself to three vital questions: What has changed? When did it change? Has it changed for the better or for the worse? The answers to these questions will help you and your supervisor in many ways, from evaluating the client's suitability for your agency to formulating diagnoses and future interventions.

Your agency may ask that you use a specific form for your mental status exam and might even require that you use the mental status exam as a formal observation tool while the client is in your office for the initial interview. If so, you should discuss with your supervisor how to introduce the idea to your client and which questions are considered vital.

As you will see from the sample questions at the end of this chapter, it is also possible to do a mental status exam without asking specific questions of the client unless something in the

---

ESSENTIAL AREAS TO ADDRESS IN THE
MENTAL STAUS EXAM

- **APPEARANCE: How does he look and behave?**
- **SPEECH: How does he speak?**
- **EMOTIONS: What is his predominant mood? What is his predominant affect? (Mood = How does the client feel *most of the time?* Affect = How does the client *appear* to be feeling *while he is with you?*)**
- **THOUGHT PROCESS AND CONTENT: (Process = *How* does the client think? Content = What does he think *about?*)**
- **SENSORY PERCEPTIONS: Are there any indications of illusions or hallucinations?**
- **MENTAL CAPACITIES: Is he oriented √6 3? What is your estimate of his intelligence? Can he remember and concentrate? How are his judgment and insight?**
- **ATTITUDE TOWARD THE INTERVIEWER: How does the client behave toward you?**

---

interview indicates a need for further information. It is always necessary that all *areas* of content be addressed (e.g., physical appearance, thought content), but there is some latitude within each area.

Regardless of when you do the mental status exam or what form you use, there are two things to keep in mind. First, if you don't understand something the client has told you, ask for a further explanation. Remember, you are embarking on a mutual effort to understand something about the client, so only rarely will the client be surprised or offended by the need for clarification. Second, your task on the mental status exam is to document what is noteworthy, and it is better—especially at the beginning—to find too much noteworthy rather than too little.

The next question is: Where to begin? The answer is always the same. No matter when you choose to do the mental status exam, you always start by describing those things about the person that anyone *looking* at him for the first time would notice, regardless of what conversation occurred. Ask yourself: What was my instantaneous visual sense of the client? Did he look healthy or sick? Did he have any obvious deformities? Was his clothing appropriate? Was it clean? Did he walk in an awkward or stiff way? Did he sit comfortably or did he seem tense? Did he have a tic? Did he look me in the eye?

There are many, many such questions. Your agency may use a standard checklist or a "fill in the blanks" form or expect you to present your mental status exam in a series of paragraphs. Whatever the format, you may wish to use the list of questions at the end of this chapter, not because an answer to every question needs to appear in your written observations about every client, but to remind yourself that, first of all, a good clinician is a good observer. Behind that statement lies a premise that *nothing* is irrelevant in understanding a client, especially at the beginning. With each successive meeting you will alter or enhance your understanding of the importance of some aspect of your first observations, but for now your radar should be scanning all the time, picking up the most obvious and the most subtle visual cues.

At the same time, however, you must continually guard against two very real temptations that arise out of the discomfort that comes from not knowing, as described in the introduction. The first is the wish to infer meaning from what you are *actually* seeing; the second is the converse of the first—that is, the temptation to "see" things that are really your own assumptions.

So how might you prematurely infer meaning from what you are seeing? Well, let's take a simple example: The client appears in a winter coat in June. That might strike you as inappropriate, even bizarre, and your inclination might be to label that observable fact as pathological and short-circuit the process of exploration necessary to discover whether it might mean something different.

For example, is the winter coat a sign of poverty? Might it signal some medical condition that needs attention? Is it covering bruises? These are only three possibilities; you can no doubt think of many more. The point, however, is that, rather than inferring from a single piece of data, you must use what you are seeing to point you in the direction of further questions for yourself and for the client.

The other pitfall in this process is to "see" things that are actually your own feelings or assumptions. For instance, the client reports to you that he is a recovering drug addict who stole money from his friends and family to support his habit. As you hear his story you can also "see" that he is humiliated by this revelation and feels he deserves to be punished. That description might be based on a series of observable cues; i.e., the client did not make eye contact during the time he was talking about his addiction *and* the client shifted in his seat *and* the client expressed difficulty in talking about his drug-related behavior because "It always makes me feel like I got away with murder." Given those observable points of reference, the assumption that the client experiences humiliation and feelings that he should be punished is demonstrable.

However, what we are concerned about guarding against in such a situation is a conclusion that the client is humiliated and deserves to be punished because if you were in his shoes that's the way *you* would feel or because, despite your good intentions as a clinician, you have some feeling that he *ought* to feel that way considering what he did to all those people who trusted him. That is, you are "seeing" something that is actually coming from you and not from the client.

So thus forewarned about what you are seeing and what you are not, you should note any visual cues that strike you as unusual. If the client offers no explanation of these signs himself, you will discuss what they might mean with your supervisor and use that discussion to focus your attention in the next interview. Or, the two of you may combine them with material from other areas of the mental status exam to begin a broader formulation.

While you are in the process of making a mental or written note to yourself of those significant visual characteristics, you should begin focusing your attention on the client's *speech*, which is the next major area of observable information to be included in the mental status exam. What is meant in the MSE by speech is *how* the client says what he says, not what he is saying. Does he say it rapidly or slowly? Does he not speak at all? Does he have an impediment to his speech that makes it difficult for him to say what he wishes to say or for you to understand it?

Does he speak audibly or are you straining to hear? Is his voice inappropriately loud? Does he talk baby-talk or speak in such a rapid, frantic way that you wonder if he could stop if he wanted to? All these are questions concerning speech, and anything that strikes you as unusual is noteworthy.

The next area of concentration will be the client's *emotions*. However, before we begin to explore this dimension of the MSE it should be mentioned that you may or may not focus your attention on these broad areas in quite such a neat series as they are being described. If you are doing the mental status exam with a questionnaire, it will almost certainly go in this order. But if you are conducting an interview from which you will do the MSE after the client leaves your office, you will probably discover that you have skipped around during your interview. The important thing is to remember that all the areas of observation are necessary in order to complete a rigorous mental status exam.

What do we mean by emotions? Well, two things. The first is *mood*, the second is *affect*, and this distinction seems to be a particularly sticky one for many clinicians. Perhaps this will help: Mood refers to how the client is *feeling most of the time*. When you ask, he may tell you. For instance, he may say, "I feel panicky all the time," or "I wake up angry, I go to work angry, I come home angry." In these cases, you would say in your description of his mood, "The client's predominant mood is one of panic (or anger)," and use the quote from the client to document that statement.

But sometimes the client has difficulty describing his mood. At these times you need to make an inference based on a combination of observable manifestations and the client's own

---

REMEMBER

- **When writing up your mental status exam, whenever possible, document your observations with the client's own words.**

comments. To minimize the possibility of misjudging the client's mood, it is best to document both your observations and his words. For example, "The client's predominant mood is depressed. He sits in a slumped position. His hair appears uncombed. He states, 'I used to come home and cook myself a real meal. Now if I can fix myself a bowl of cereal it's a big deal.' 'I can't remember the last time I slept through the night.' 'The guys at work keep asking me where my head is at these days.'"

Two final comments about mood before we go on to affect. First, note carefully that you are doing nothing more here than giving a name to the most pervasive internal state the client is experiencing and documenting the evidence for that state. You are not speculating on *why* the client feels that way; you are simply noting it. Second, there are many mood states other than anxiety or depression. People feel scared, or overwhelmed, or elated, or restless, or tense, or lots of other things. Try to find the most accurate description you can for what the client is experiencing.

Now to the question of affect. Affect refers to the way the client *shows* his emotions while he is with you, and it may or may not coincide with the internal state the client describes himself as feeling over time. That idea should become clearer as we examine the various aspects of assessing the client's affect, so let's start with the first question you ask yourself: What is the predominant affective state of this client? You may not be able to answer the question entirely until the interview is over; however, what you want to know is: How did this client *look and sound* most of the time he was with me, *regardless of his underlying mood?* For example, did he sound confident, or worried, or angry, or sad most of the interview? If so, that's how you would describe his predominant affect. For instance, "The client's predominant affect was defiant. He repeatedly stated his belief that 'I never needed my wife to begin with' and 'If he wants her he can have her' in a defiant tone of voice."

Next you would note the *variability* of his affect. To use the abovementioned example: Does he look and sound defiant even when he's talking about things other than his faltering relationship with his wife? If so, there's not much variability in his affect, and that should be noted.

You also want to attend to the *intensity* of a client's affect. Does it seem excessive in any direction? Does he shout or sob uncontrollably through most of the interview or, conversely, does he speak in a lifeless, unemotional way? This latter phenomenon is noted as *blunted* or *flat* affect, depending on its severity.

Next you want to notice how *labile* the affect is. Does the client's expression of his feelings shift rapidly from laughing to crying, from intense rage to a sense of calm amusement? Do you experience a sense that this person is on an emotional rollercoaster? If so, you would describe this client's affect as very labile, and you would give a description of what you observed during the interview that documented that lability.

Finally, you describe your observations about the *appropriateness* of the client's affect to the content of the interview. Obvious examples of the inappropriateness of affect would be a person who giggles while he is telling you he was assaulted last week or cries as he describes the woman of his dreams. In either case you would note that the affect seemed inappropriate to the content and cite an example wherever possible.

No doubt, in reading these distinctions of variability or lability or intensity, you are concerned with what seem like too subtle differences between various aspects of assessing a client's affect. In fact, however, with practice they begin to leap out at you. And, as with all other categories of the mental status examination, you will not necessarily comment on each aspect of affect in every write-up. The important thing is to note those things that seem particularly distinctive or out of the ordinary.

Once you have done that it is time to turn your attention to the client's *thoughts*, focusing first on the *process* of the thoughts and then on the *content*. In order to orient yourself to these different aspects of thought, it will help to remember that process is *how a person thinks* and content is *what a person thinks about*. A songwriter might say that process is the music and content is the words.

How would you recognize something notable in a client's thought process? Well, he may describe it to you. He may say that his thoughts go too fast for him or "they seem all jumbled up" or that it seems like he can hardly think at all, suggesting that his thoughts might actually be moving more slowly than usual. If he describes some aspect of his thought processes, write it down.

But what if he doesn't? Well, you're going to get some sense of the way he thinks by the way he talks, and your own reactions as the client is talking may help alert you to something unusual. For instance, if you ask the client a question and you find yourself thinking "get to the point" while he is responding, the client may be demonstrating *circumstantiality*. This is a disturbance in thought processes which is characterized by a lack of goal direction, although the person eventually gets to your question. Obviously, you have to ask yourself whether you frequently feel people should get to the point more rapidly before you put such a description in the mental status exam; however, if this reaction is unusual for you, then it is probably objectively unusual.

You may also hear certain words being uttered over and over again, regardless of what you have said. For example, the client may keep repeating "yes, yes, quite, quite" while you are talking or as a response, no matter what the content. This is called *perseveration* and can be a repeated phrase, such as was just described, or a return to the same subject no matter what efforts you make to divert him. In either case, you will have a sense that the client *has* to keep repeating that expression, rather than choosing it because of the content you are discussing.

The next area of attention involving thought processes is that of *associations*. There are a number of different aspects to the question of how a client makes associations in his thinking, but the basic question is: How does the client get from one idea to the next? This may sound subtle, but you can frequently tell that you are in the presence of someone who is having difficulty with associations if you find yourself thinking while he is talking "What?" or "Did I miss something?" or "I don't get it" or any similar thought suggesting that you are having difficulty following his train of thought.

Obviously, you are going to first ask yourself whether you *did* miss something. Was your mind wandering or were you momentarily distracted by some interruption? But if you repeatedly have this experience, you may be in the presence of one of a number of phenomena involving associations. The most frequently encountered are *tangentiality*, *loose associations*, and *flight of ideas*.

When someone's thinking is *tangential*, you may very well have the sensation that he is *sort of* talking about the subject at hand, but not quite. For instance, if you ask him about his job, he may tell you about people looking for jobs in today's difficult economic times or some other response that is about jobs but doesn't answer the question. If that happens only when you ask about his job, then you might need to understand more about the sensitivity this client feels about discussing his work situation. If it is tangentiality, it will recur with other topics as well.

So will *loose associations*, a term which means simply that the client moves from one topic to another without any apparent connection between the two. You may recognize this when you find yourself struggling to "fill in the blanks." For example, consider the verse "roses are red, violets are blue, I like chop suey, do you smoke?" If you hear two unrelated ideas, like those last two lines, and you find yourself thinking, "Let's see, he was in a Chinese restaurant and someone near him was smoking . . . ," then you are experiencing the disturbance of thought process known as loose associations.

Finally, there is *flight of ideas*, which is aptly named because it often is accompanied by rapid speech, so that you literally feel like you are "flying" with such a client. However, it can occasionally occur without rapid speech and might just feel like "free associating," which most of us can do when we're asked. The difference for someone with flight of ideas is that he cannot stop doing it.

There are other disturbances of thought processes, but once you begin to listen for how people string ideas together you will certainly notice any significant difficulty. If you're not sure it falls in any of the categories described, simply note in your mental status exam that "the client appears to experience a disruption in his thought processes." You and your supervisor can then explore the specifics together.

Once you have done that, you can turn your attention to the *content* of the client's thoughts. This area of exploration is aimed at discovering the answers to a series of questions: What does the client think is going on around him? What role does he play in it? And what role do other people play in relationship to him? If any of the answers demonstrate serious distortions in the client's thoughts, you are likely to be hearing a *delusion*, which, simply stated, is an idea about one of these questions that the client absolutely believes to be true and you know absolutely to be untrue in reality. However, we are not talking here about who won the World Series in 1958 or whether the federal government is really closing an historic monument.

We *are* talking, for example, about a client who suggests that he has unusual or magical or mystical or exaggerated powers. He may tell you directly that he is God, or Napoleon, or some other famous powerful person, or he may simply allude to extraordinary capacities. In either case, you will want first to ask a few broad questions and then to ask directly about these ideas to elicit some sense of the depth of the client's beliefs. If he is clearly convinced of these rare powers, you are in the presence of someone who is suffering from *delusions of grandeur.*

Or he may tell you that someone or some organization "is out to get me" or has already attempted to hurt him in some way or another. He may tell you he is being followed by agents from the Internal Revenue Service or by a woman who sold him bus tokens last week. Often, if you are having difficulty knowing whether the person might be describing a situation in which he is really in danger, you can ask whether he has gone to the police. Depending on the clarity and reasonableness of his answer, you will probably have a clue as to whether he experiences *delusions of persecution.*

Somewhat akin to this are *thought broadcasting*, which is an unshakable belief that other people can read his mind or hear what he is thinking, and *ideas of reference*, in which the client believes that insignificant or unrelated events in the world have some secret meaning aimed at him. For example, he will show you what appears to be a perfectly ordinary classified advertisement and tell you that it is in code from his counterpart in a spy ring or that the Pope is trying to communicate with him.

Or the client might suffer from *delusions of control*, in which he believes that something or someone other than himself may be controlling what he does or says or thinks or that he can do this to others. Although it may sometimes be hard to differentiate the latter from delusions of grandeur, the idea that *he* is being controlled is often evident because the client frequently believes it is a machine or mechanical device of some sort that is controlling him. For example, your client may tell you that his answering machine tells him when to make phone calls or that the computers at his office are causing him to do things he should not be doing.

Lastly, there are *somatic delusions*, which can sometimes be difficult to distinguish from severe anxiety about one's health or physical well-being. In this case, you will simply have to patiently pursue a series of questions to find out whether or not the person's fear that he has some deadly disease or unusual condition is based in reality. You will get some help in this regard when you receive pertinent medical records.

Delusions are not the only manifestations of a disturbance in thinking which you may encounter. Sometimes it will seem to you as if a client cannot let go of an idea. In fact, he may report to you that over and over again he keeps on having a thought that he doesn't understand the origin of or wishes would go away, but cannot stop himself from thinking no matter what he does. This unremitting experience of an unwanted thought is known as an *obsession*. You may have heard this term used interchangeably with a *compulsion*, but they are not the same. Probably the easiest way to remember the distinction is that an obsession is *always* a thought and a compulsion is *always* a deed.

For example, a person may describe to you a recurrent thought that his mother is going to drown. That is an obsession. However, along with that persistent thought he may describe suffering a repeated behavior which he does not want to do, knows is unnecessary, and yet cannot stop. For example, he may tell you it takes him an hour to take a shower because he has to count all the tiles in the shower three times before he can turn the water on or off. He will probably be embarrassed and humiliated to tell you this, and may say that he thinks it is crazy, but he must do it. This is a compulsion.

Most compulsive rituals cluster around one of three types of actions: repetitive cleaning or washing, most often of one's hands; or checking, such as returning to one's house many times to make sure the gas is off or the lights turned out; or counting, such as the incident described above with the bathroom tiles. They are not, technically, a disturbance of thought, but so often accompany obsessions that one should always inquire about one if the other is present.

The client may also experience obsessive thoughts that arouse intense fears. These are known as *phobias*. They may be of specific situations, such as riding elevators or crossing bridges, or they may be more global, such as a fear of leaving one's house, known as agoraphobia, or a fear of heights, known as acrophobia, or a fear of strangers, known as xenophobia, or any one of a number of others.

Finally, there are disturbances of thought related to the idea of killing oneself or someone else. These are referred to in clinical parlance as *suicidal* or *homicidal ideation*. Needless to say, these areas of assessment are critical, and can cause extraordinary anxiety for the clinician, so they will be taken up separately in Chapters Eight and Nine.

Once you have noted any relevant observations about the process and content of the client's thoughts, you should turn your attention to any unusual aspects of his sensory perceptions. These divide themselves into two categories: *illusions* or *hallucinations*. Illusions refer to normal sensory events that are misperceived. For example, the wind blows a curtain in your office and the client tells you that it is a vampire coming through the window. If it is apparent that he is convinced of this fact, you are witnessing an illusion.

If, on the other hand, the client reports an experience involving one of the five senses, unrelated to any external stimuli and clearly not true, that is an hallucination. For example, he may say that he hears his dead sister's voice telling him to join her (an auditory hallucination), or sees the devil beckoning to him (a visual hallucination), or smells flesh rotting (an olfactory hallucination). Auditory and visual hallucinations are the most common. Olfactory, tactile (involving the belief that one is being touched by something or someone), and gustatory (that something is being tasted) hallucinations are very unusual.

One of the last areas of concern in any thorough mental status exam involves some assessment of fundamental *mental capacities*. The first involves *orientation*. If you have ever read a mental status exam, you may have come across a bewildering expression that "the client is oriented x 3." The three orientations referred to are *time, place, and person*. Assuming that the person you are interviewing speaks your language reasonably well, you ought, without having to ask, to be certain by the end of your time together that he knows approximately what time of day it is, what day of the week it is, and what year it is. He ought to be able to tell you where he is and what his name is. You will almost certainly know this about the client, but if you have any doubts by all means ask, since a statement about orientation is essential.

Second would be an observation about the client's *level of intelligence*. What you would indicate here is a simple assessment of whether or not you feel that the client possesses at least average intelligence or above or whether you feel that his intelligence might be below average.

Next you would ask yourself about the client's capacity for *concentration*. Can he pay attention reasonably well to the subject you are discussing? Is he easily distracted? If this is an area of serious doubt on your part, you can ask the client to count backwards from 20 or to subtract from 100 by threes. Assuming the client understands subtraction, you can use either of these tests to inform yourself of his ability to concentrate, since interference with this capacity will be readily demonstrated by confusion or simply forgetting his place.

Clearly linked to the capacity for concentration is *memory* functioning. Does the person remember what happened yesterday (recent memory) but not significant facts from when he was a ten-year-old boy, such as the name of the town he lived in or who was President (remote memory)? Is the opposite true? Or does he have difficulty remembering the name of a significant person he talked about ten minutes ago (immediate memory)? Any or all of these should be noted.

The last areas of intellectual functioning you would comment upon are the client's *judgment* and capacity for *insight*. A concern about the client's judgment may arise at any point in the interview. For instance, he may tell you that he frequently initiates fist fights in bars, or steals cars, or beats his children. Any dangerous or impulsive or violent behavior would be described as poor or impaired judgment on the mental status exam and should include examples. If you sense some possible impairment of a client's judgment but it is never raised in the interview, ask a question such as, "What would you do if you saw someone get hurt?" or "smelled smoke in a movie theatre that was filled with people?"

Insight refers to whether or not a person understands that he has a problem. How does he understand his problem and how does he describe it? For instance, is it outside of him (e.g. "Everybody always blames me for things")? Does he wish help for himself? If so, why now? And is what he wishes help with a reasonably accurate perception of what might be the problem he is having? Can he describe anything about his feeling states?

Answers to any of these questions should lead you to an estimate of his capacity for insight, although it is important to remember that a limited capacity in an initial interview does not mean a person is necessarily a poor candidate for therapy, since he simply may not understand that talking about one's feelings is okay here.

Finally, having completed your comments about the client's mental capacities, you are going to devote the last part of your mental status exam to commenting on the client's *attitude toward you, the interviewer.* Does he seem suspicious or uncooperative? Afraid or arrogant? Reserved or flamboyantly trying to entertain you? And, most importantly, does the client seem to have an interest or ability to form an alliance with you to work on the shared task of understanding his problem? He may or he may not; in either case, it requires an observation. And when you have completed that task, you will have completed your first mental status exam.

However, by now at least two things are probably happening: first, a conviction that producing such a document would take months, and second, a feeling that descriptions of some of the possible client behaviors or ideas sound crazy and would scare you out of your wits if you actually came face-to-face with them.

Let's start with the latter concern first, for it is certainly the place in which *your* feelings count most in doing a mental status exam. If what you are hearing or seeing makes you feel endangered, or as if this client is out of touch with reality or might hurt himself or someone else, there are concise appropriate steps that you can take to reassure both yourself and the client. These procedures will be addressed in Chapters Eight and Nine.

As to the question of whether or not you will ever really be able to do a reasonably competent, reasonably speedy mental status exam, suffice it to say that it does take time and practice, that the first few you do will seem very laborious, that you will not remember the names or differences between things for a while—and that eventually you will get the hang of it.

OUTLINE FOR A MENTAL STATUS EXAM

Below are the *general areas of observation* on which you should focus while the client is with you, and document after the interview, to produce a complete mental status exam. Wherever possible and appropriate, you should use the client's own words to augment your observations.

The mental status exam is also a useful tool for assessing children; however, it must be adapted to their developmental level. You should discuss with your supervisor how to do that.

APPEARANCE

1. Does the client look healthy?
2. Does he look his age? If not, does he appear older or younger?
3. Does he have any obvious physical deformities? Describe.
4. Is he appropriately dressed?
5. Is his clothing clean?
6. Does he walk or move in an unusual way?
7. Does he sit in a comfortable posture?
8. Does he have any visible scars?
9. Do his height and weight appear to be appropriate?
10. Does he have any visible tics or unusual movements of the body, face, or eyes?
11. Does he make eye contact? If so, consistently or intermittently?
12. What is the client's facial expression? Does it change over the course of the interview?

SPEECH

1. Does the client speak?
2. Does he speak unusually rapidly or slowly?
3. Does he have a speech impediment?
4. Does he speak unusually loudly or softly?

EMOTIONS

1. What is the client's predominant mood? Describe the comments and behavior on which you base this observation.
2. What is his predominant affect? Describe the comments and behavior on which you base this observation.
3. Does his affect vary over the course of the interview?
4. Does his affect seem excessive at any time? Describe.
5. Does he exhibit labile affect?
6. Is his affect appropriate to the content of the interview?

THOUGHT PROCESSES AND CONTENT

1. Is the client's thought process circumstantial?
2. Is it perseverative?
3. Is his thinking tangential?
4. Does he demonstrate loose associations or flight of ideas?
5. Does he exhibit somatic delusions, or delusions of grandeur, persecution, or control? On what comments do you base this observation?

(*continued*)

6. Does he appear to exhibit thought broadcasting or ideas of reference? On what comments do you base this observation?
7. Does he suffer obsessive thoughts or experience compulsive behavior? If so, describe.
8. Is he phobic? If so, what is the nature of the phobia?
9. Are there indications of homicidal or suicidal ideation? If so, on what comments do you base this observation?
10. Is there a particular subject that seems to preoccupy the client's thoughts? If so, describe.

SENSORY PERCEPTION

1. Does the client appear to have any hearing problems?
2. Does the client appear to have any sight problems?
3. Does the client suffer from illusions or hallucinations? If so, are the latter auditory, visual, olfactory, tactile, or gustatory? On what comments or behavior do you base this observation?

MENTAL CAPACITIES

1. Is the client oriented to time, place, and person?
2. Does the client appear to be of average intelligence or above?
3. Does he exhibit a capacity for concentration within the normal range?
4. Does he exhibit appropriate recent, remote, and immediate memory? If not, on what do you base this observation?
5. Does his judgment appear impaired in any way? If so, on what comments or behavior do you base this observation?
6. Does he have an appropriate sense of self-worth? If not, on what comments or behavior do you base this observation?
7. Does he appear to understand the consequences of his behavior?
8. Does he exhibit a capacity for insight?

ATTITUDE TOWARD THE INTERVIEWER

1. What is the client's attitude toward you?
2. Does it change over the course of the interview?
3. Does he respond to empathy?
4. Does he appear to be capable of empathy?

The Mental Status Exam: A Sample

Below is an example of a mental status exam written following the first interview with Angel G. at the SouthWest Mental Health Clinic. Mr. G. came with concerns about caring for his family after being laid off recently from his job.

> Angel G. is a thin, neatly dressed Hispanic male who appeared younger than his stated age of 39. He sat stiffly throughout the interview and made only intermittent eye-contact. His right hand continually tapped the chair. Mr. G.'s speech was rapid and loud. His predominant mood was anxious. He stated, "I don't sleep. All night I'm thinking and thinking. What if I don't find anything?" Mr. G.'s predominant affect was fearfulness but did vary with the content of the interview and was not notably labile or inappropriate. He described his thoughts as "racing all the time lately," but evidenced no thought disorder. His thoughts are preoccupied with fears he may lose his wife and children. Mr. G. denies any suicidal or homicidal ideation and shows no evidence of illusions or hallucinations. He is oriented x 3 and is of average intelligence or above. He states, "I forget all the time. Like I'm going crazy or something. I never forgot anything before." Mr. G.'s judgment appears somewhat impaired regarding his fears that his family might leave him. "Last week I could not let my children go to school. I thought if they went I would never see them again." He has a capacity for insight and stated, "My father lost his job and my mother took us away. I think this has something to do with that." Mr. G. related to the interviewer in an alternately guarded and self-deprecating way, stating several times, "I don't like talking about this. Probably you can't do much for somebody like me."

three

How to Think About Your Client's Health: The Medical History

Having now threaded your way through your first mental status exam, you are enhancing your skills of observation, listening with a greater sense of what you should be listening for, and honing your descriptive language to more accurately communicate to others what you have seen and heard. In short, you are focusing intently on *all* the expressions of your client's emotions. Right? Well, not quite.

So what's missing, you ask? And what on earth would thinking about a client's medical history have to do with it? Why would it be your job anyway? After all, you're interested in becoming an accomplished clinician who devotes time and effort to helping clients understand their *feelings*.

The short answer is that thinking and asking about the client's physical health might turn out to be one of the most important things you ever do with that client. The long answer is this chapter, the purpose of which is to help you appreciate the profound interrelationship between psyche (mind) and soma (body) and to elaborate on the basic premise that a good, responsible clinician thinks, asks, and demonstrates concern about her client's physical well-being.

As with all other aspects of assessment, when and what you should ask about the client's health will vary depending on the setting in which you work and the circumstances under which the client comes for treatment. If you work in a hospital, you may very well have a full medical workup available to you before you ever meet the client, as well as an opportunity to consult with her medical doctor. If you are in an outpatient setting such as a community mental health clinic, there may be a form routinely signed by each new client that gives permission to contact her medical doctor and/or a brief medical history that the patient herself fills out prior to being seen for the first time.

If the client has filled out such a form, read it carefully. Has she answered all the questions? If not, is the lapse related to language or unfamiliarity with the terms, or should you wonder if she has chosen not to answer particular questions? Perhaps she skipped the section related to drug or alcohol consumption because she does not yet feel comfortable telling you about her worry that she may be a substance abuser. Or maybe she indicated that her brother died at age 26 but did not indicate the cause of death. If so, you might eventually find out that he committed suicide and she is too frightened or embarrassed to offer that information. Or the absence of data may be related to that particular client's cultural attitudes or personal feelings about "doctors" (regardless of your actual professional training, you may often be perceived and addressed as "doctor").

If the client has not filled out such a form, you need to discuss with your supervisor whether your agency has any procedure or policy regarding the necessity of acquiring such information. If there is a policy, when should you act on it? Some believe it is essential to ask at least some broad questions about health issues in the initial interview, so that that information can be brought to the treatment team; others feel that the client could be put off by that and recommend that you simply let the information emerge over time. In either case, whatever does emerge in your interviews should be noted in detail and shared with the treatment team.

In clinical work, as has been stated before, there is a great temptation to *prematurely* ascribe psychodynamic or cognitive or contextual meaning to a client's behaviors and interactions. Even though those ascriptions may eventually turn out to be very insightful, this is a dangerous business. The reason one is so tempted is probably obvious to you. After all, understanding the meaning of behavior is part of what makes this work so interesting and gratifying. The reason it is dangerous might not be so obvious: Where your client works or how she makes love, what kind of food she likes or how she gets along with her siblings, how she sleeps at night and whether she remembers her umbrella when she leaves your office might just as conceivably turn out to be symptoms of a physical illness as they are of an emotional conflict or a need to rethink behavior.

Thousands of years of folk medicine and hundreds of years of modern science have amply documented the truth that there is hardly a system of the body - be it respiratory, or cardiovascular, or endocrine, or any other-that cannot be altered, however briefly or benignly, by feelings. But it is equally well documented that it is the rare "behavioral problem" or "mood swing" or symptom of "anxiety" or "depression" that is not also a potential symptom of disease in the organism. For example, consider "the mad hatter" in *Alice in Wonderland*. We think of him as some daffy eccentric who came from Lewis Carroll's fertile imagination. In fact, in the nineteenth century hatters used a form of mercury to cure the felt from which they made their creations, and breathing mercury fumes day in and day out produced real changes in the brain chemistry that were often accompanied by noticeably peculiar behavior. In Lewis Carroll's time, such people were described as "mad." Today we might say there were "profound neurological sequelae produced by toxins in the work environment." The point remains the same: The *appearance* of a mental disorder may be a *symptom*, not the cause of your client's suffering.

How your client makes love-or her lack of desire to do so-may have more to do with a pill she is taking for her diabetes than it does with her belief that her husband is unfaithful to her. A loss of appetite "even for my favorite foods" may signal a depressive reaction to a real event, just as the client says it does. But it might also be linked to an underlying medical condition-for example, the presence of the HIV virus-which is *both* making the client experience feelings of hopelessness *and* causing her body to be unable to metabolize food normally. A client's report that "I hit my sister for no reason" may indicate a lifelong pattern of poor impulse control and sibling rivalry or it may be a symptom of a brain tumor.

By now you have probably gotten the idea. No doubt, you

could formulate your own ideas as to how a change in sleep habits or memory functioning—even forgetting an umbrella in your office—might be significant. And by now you can also see that it would be a dangerous conceit to presume that all problems can be cured by talking about feelings or changing behavior. So let's proceed to some of the basic questions you need to think about related to your client's physical health and medical history.

First, does the client bring up any concerns about her health on her own? If so, how does she see their relationship to her presenting problem? For example, does the client tell you she is here because she recently discovered that she has high blood pressure and that since that discovery she is constantly fearful that she is going to die? If so, she is experiencing the medical problem as the stressor that is *causing* the feeling. Or she may report that she has always had trouble working for other people but that lately when she has an encounter with her boss she feels dizziness and nausea for hours afterwards. In that case, she is concerned that it is her *feelings* that are precipitating a health problem.

In either case, she has provided you with an opportunity to further discuss her health, because she herself has raised the possibility that there is a relationship between the physical symptoms and the feeling states she is experiencing. However, she has also provided you with an "opportunity" to confirm or deny her interpretation of what her physical symptoms mean. This is not your job, especially with physical symptoms. It is your job to get some factual information. It is her physician's job—perhaps in consultation with you, perhaps not—to diagnose medical conditions and to rule out physical illness.

So why bother getting this information if discovering its meaning is not your job? For one thing, aspects of a client's health history may indicate whether or not she is suitable for your clinical setting. For example, does a client have a serious enough medical condition that she might be better served at a clinic associated with a medical center, where more consistent monitoring of her health is possible? This is probably not a question you can or should answer on your own, so you will need to gather data to share with your supervisor. The two of you will then decide whether the situation needs to be discussed with someone more familiar with medical issues, such as your staff psychiatrist. (Remember, psychiatrists are trained as physicians before they are trained as psychiatrists.)

The basic concept of evaluating health factors in assessing suitability for treatment is also important because of the nature of the therapeutic process itself. That is, even though the eventual outcome of treatment may be the relief of stress, the *process* of therapy itself creates its own stress—which can sometimes be quite intense. Your information-gathering helps you and those with whom you consult to assess whether the organism itself is durable enough at this time to embark on the particular kind of treatment that your agency offers.

So let's go back to thinking about the basic information you need to ascertain the client's current state of health. If the client has raised a health problem or symptom on her own, try to answer three fundamental questions: How long has the client been experiencing this problem or symptom? How often does she experience this problem or symptom? And lastly, when she experiences the problem or symptom, how much does it interfere with her daily life?

But what if the client doesn't tell you she's having a physical problem? In fact, she may not mention her health at all. That may be a clue to you that this client is unfamiliar with the notion that body and mind are intimately intertwined. Eventually you may want to explain that concept and explore it with her. Or it may turn out to be an illustration of another fundamental premise in clinical interviewing: that what the client does not talk about may be just as important, *or more so*, in your understanding of that person as what she does share with you.

IF A CLIENT HAS A PHYSICAL SYMPTOM

- **How long has she had it?**
- **How often does it occur?**
- **How much does it interfere with her daily life?**
- **Has she seen a doctor?**

We have already touched upon some possible subjects, such as drug addiction or a family suicide, which-regardless of whether you agree with society's attitude toward them—might be hard for people to discuss.

People's health issues also carry very personal meaning. Clients may experience all health professionals—including mental health professionals—as healers or helpers; but they might just as possibly have their own reasons to believe we're intrusive or unfeeling. They may believe that the illness their great-grandmother died of is what's really causing these headaches; that you couldn't possibly help them overcome this incurable disease; that God will punish them if they talk about their pain with a stranger.

You cannot know these feelings when the client walks through your door. Nevertheless, you should not avoid talking about the client's health, even if she does not bring it up. However, you must be sensitive to the possibility that raising the issue may arouse discomfort or fear in your client.

Once the subject has been raised and you have established how troublesome or longstanding any of the client's problems or symptoms are, you will want to know if she has been to a doctor for this condition. Implicit in that question, and in her response, is another question: How do you know you have this condition? Did a doctor diagnose the symptoms or did a friend tell her, "Well, it must be thus-and-so because I had the same symptoms about five years ago," or did the client diagnose herself? Her answer may tell you a great deal not only about this client's feelings about "doctors" but also about how she views her symptoms and how she feels about taking care of herself and letting others take care of her. In addition, you may get an indication of potential difficulties in engaging this client in therapy.

If you ask the client if she has been to a doctor she may just come right out and tell you she hates doctors or her family never goes to doctors or she's afraid of doctors or she can't afford it or any of a hundred other responses. These may or may not only be feelings about the medical profession; they may also be veiled ways of expressing a worry that she may need to be hospitalized or have some painful procedure; they may even be an indirect communication about how she feels about seeing you at this moment or what she imagines therapy will be like (e.g., anxiety-producing or too expensive or too intrusive or against the grain of what her family has told her about the "right way" to handle one's problems).

Clearly, it is not your job to try and talk any client out of her feelings, either about a medical checkup or about therapy, but it may be necessary—if your agency *does* require it—to explain to the client that getting a medical checkup is a routine part of the intake procedure here, and then to discuss with her when and how she might go about doing that. Again, how firmly you adhere to that expectation should be discussed with your supervisor.

Once you have established who diagnosed the condition, you will want to explore whether or not the client is taking any medications for it. These may be medications prescribed by her doctor or they may be over-the-counter remedies such as cough medicines or pills to inhibit water retention, etc. Whatever they are, you want to know how often and how much she takes. Is that a dosage the doctor recommended? How long has she been taking them and is she aware of any side-effects they may be causing? If you've never heard of the medication, ask her to spell it for you. If she can't spell it and you've never heard of it, perhaps she has the bottle with her and you can copy the name. Then find out what that particular medication is supposed to do and whether or not she thinks it is helping.

The issue of medication is an extremely complicated one.

IF A CLIENT IS TAKING MADICATION

- **Was it prescribed?**
- **If so, by whom?**
- **Why was it prescribed?**
- **What is it called?**
- **How much is she taking?**
- **How often is she taking it?**
- **Is it helping?**

There are literally hundreds of medications prescribed for common medical conditions (e.g., allergies, asthma, high blood pressure) which have known side-effects related to changes in mood. No one would expect you to be familiar with the side-effects of every drug on the market for every condition, but the knowledge that your client is taking a particular medication will make it possible for you to explore with her physician or your staff psychiatrist its potential relationship to the changes in mood or behavior the client is experiencing. However, even if the medication is not known to affect mood, it could still be having that effect on your client, since every person taking a medication has her own unique reaction to it.

It is especially important, therefore, to think about basic issues, such as age, size, and present life circumstances, when you are discussing a client's current medications with the treatment team. The same dosage of medication can have very different effects on an 89-year-old and a 45-year-old. If a child is taking a particular medication this may be an indicator of a much more serious condition than if an adult were taking the same drug. A client may tell you she is taking her pills three times a day, but if she lives alone and is feeling depressed she may inadvertently be taking five pills one day and none the next.

Another reason to inquire about medications the client is taking is that the medication itself may be masking some other condition, either medical or psychological. This could be something as routine as the client taking over-the-counter medications for a stuffy nose: If the stuffy nose has returned every time she stops the medication and that pattern has been going on for six months, then some further exploration might be indicated to see if the symptom is being caused by some underlying medical condition which, although it might not be serious, should be addressed so that the client can have some relief.

Or more serious implications might be suggested. For instance, the client might be taking over-the-counter medication to help her sleep and may have done so for years without ever telling her doctor. That could be contributing to a physical problem she is having; or it might be the only way she can manage overwhelming nighttime anxiety; or it might be a subtle disguise for a suicidal wish to "sleep forever" rather than tolerate another night of thinking about her problems.

So the client may intentionally or unintentionally be using a medication that is affecting her mood. There are also medications that are given *deliberately* to alter mood or behavior; these are known as psychotropic medications. These can cause physical symptoms as diverse as seizures, headaches, tremors, etc. In some instances, prolonged use may even produce irreversible side effects. For this and many other reasons, the use of psychotropic medications has often been a source of controversy among clinicians. Some argue that medication inhibits the progress of treatment; others view these drugs as a revolutionary advance in the relief of mental suffering; still others find them a necessary and suitable adjunct to therapy for certain conditions.

Whatever position you or your agency might be inclined to take regarding psychotropic medications, as a responsible clinician you do have an obligation to at least familiarize yourself with the names and basic characteristics of the major categories (tranquilizers, antidepressants, antipsychotics, etc.). Again, this information will be helpful in determining the client's suitability for your clinic, since it may give you a measure of the severity and duration of a mental condition that would indicate a need for a more or less structured treatment setting than the one in which you work. Or it may suggest the need for a different sort of intervention altogether, such as a job training program or a group living situation.

Another reason to pursue information about the kind of psychotropic medication the client is taking is because *someone* is prescribing it for her. That doctor may be a psychiatrist who is monitoring the client's use of that antianxiety medication on a monthly basis. But it could also be a doctor in a local emergency room who gave the client a short supply of medication with the understanding that whatever agency she went to next would take over responsibility for continuing the medication. Or it might be the family doctor, who actually prescribed that antidepressant for the client's sister, who never took it. Whatever the circumstances under which the client got the medication, you need to ascertain whether or not her expectation, or her doctor's expectation, is that your clinic will now assume responsibility for evaluating the ongoing need for medication and for providing it. This may or may not be a service your agency is willing or able to provide, so you will need to discuss this question with the treatment team.

Once you have clarified whether or not your client is using any medications—either psychotropics or medicine for a current medical condition—you will want to get at least a thumbnail sketch of her medical history. Is this a person who has been basically healthy up until recently, or does she have a history of chronic or debilitating conditions dating back to childhood? Did a serious illness or physical problem occur at a particularly crucial time in her development? For example, you may find out that she had a burn on her face when she was six that now looks fine, after several operations and plastic surgery, but was disfiguring then, or that during adolescence she had a broken back that required six months of being away from school and friends. Remember, it is not your purpose at this stage to explore the *meaning* of these events with the client. You are simply gathering data and listening for any indications of their meaning to her. As with all the other information you are gathering about the client, after she has left you will want to think about her history and what it might represent to her.

Lastly, it is a good idea to briefly explore her family's medical history. Who died when and of what? Was it a lingering illness and who took care of the sick person? How old was the client when that person died and what was his or her significance in the client's life? There are many such questions, and by now you will no doubt be thinking about what various answers might mean to your client.

For example, the death of a mother while she was giving birth to a younger sibling when your client was two will have very different implications from the death of a mother who killed herself when your client was 12. A 49-year-old client who recently lost a 54-year-old sister to ovarian cancer will feel very differently about it if hers is the third generation of women in her family who succumbed to ovarian cancer in their fifties than if no one in the family ever had that illness before.

The examples are legion, as are the feelings and meanings about health and illness that each client brings to therapy. Every subculture has its own beliefs and traditions; every family's attitudes and behaviors are different; every client has cul-

---

Symptoms of HIV

- Many of these symptoms can also be associated with illnesses *other* than HIV. Nevertheless, you should be familiar with and alert to the following:

- General symptoms of HIV which may appear in men, women and children include dramatic weight loss, chronic swollen glands, skin rashes, persistent diarrhea, chronic herpes, bronchial pneumonia, recurrent minor infections, flu-like symptoms, tuberculosis, persistent coughing, shingles, thrush, and constant fatigue.

- In women, HIV may also manifest itself in symptoms such as anemia, urinary tract infections, vaginal warts or ulcers, chronic vaginal yeast infections, cervical cancer or irregular pap smears, or any chronic gynecological problem. Symptoms often appear first during pregnancy.

- In children, the presence of HIV may also be indicated by recurring fevers, breathing difficulties, "failure-to-thrive" syndrome, developmental delays, brain damage, or chronic ear, nose and throat problems.

---

tural and family beliefs and feelings superimposed over her own individual sensibilities. And they may all be very different from yours.

You must strike a balance between the role of responsible clinician who requires certain information in order to assess what will really be most helpful and that of respectful interviewer who will patiently seek to understand the client's attitudes and meanings better before asking questions that may feel too intrusive or irrelevant to her. Once you have the data, you will do what you always do with new information: Write it down, and after the client leaves, think about it.

THE MEDICAL HISTORY

Below is a series of questions to which you *eventually* should know the answers about a client. They are not necessarily questions you will ask the client directly; rather, they indicate information for which you should be listening. If it is necessary to ask the client these questions, the order and time at which they will be introduced should be discussed with your supervisor.

1. How is the client's health? Is this a change?
2. When was the last time she saw a doctor? For what reason?
3. Does she have regular checkups?
4. Does she smoke?
5. Does she drink? What does she drink? How much? How often?
6. Has she ever used any illegal drugs? Which ones? How often? For how long? Did she ever use any drugs intravenously?

If the client reports a current health problem:

7. When did this problem/condition start?
8. How often does it happen?
9. When it happens, how much does it interfere with her everyday life?
10. Has she seen a doctor for this problem?
11. Has she ever been hospitalized for this problem or some other problem?
12. If so, when, and for how long?
13. Does the client take any medication that is prescribed? What for? For how long? What is the dosage? Has she noticed any side-effects?
14. Does she take any over-the-counter medications on a regular basis? For what purpose? How often? How much? Has she noticed any sideeffects?
15. Has the client ever had any significant difficulties with a lack of sexual desire? Lack of arousal or erection? Lack of sexual satisfaction?
16. Has the client ever been pregnant? Were there any complications?
17. Has the client ever been tested for AIDS? Has the client ever thought she should be tested for AIDS? If so, why?
18. Does the client have any historical factors that put her at risk for AIDS, such as intravenous drug use that included sharing of needles, prostitution, blood transfusions prior to the discovery of the AIDS virus, unprotected sexual activity with a homosexual, bisexual, or heterosexual partner?
19. Does the client have, or has she had, any physical symptoms that suggest the presence of the HIV virus?

Other History:

20. Did she have any health problems as a child?
21. Was hospitalization or surgery ever necessary?
22. Has she ever had any serious accidents?
23. Are both her parents living? If not, what was the cause of death?
24. Are her brothers and/or sisters still alive? If not, what was the cause of death? If so, how is their health?
25. Does the client have children? If so, are they still alive? How is their health? If not, what was the cause of death?

four

HOW TO CONDUCT THE FIRST
INTERVIEW WITH A FAMILY

In almost any agency or institution, it is highly likely that you will be seeing families from time to time. However, "seeing families" is not the same as doing family therapy. You may occasionally meet with a child's entire family in order to get a sense of his day-to-day life. You may see parents for guidance about handling particular problems in the family. You will certainly see families if you are working in a foster care or child welfare agency. If you work in a medical setting, you may meet with a family to discuss issues concerning the hospitalization or medical treatment of one member. These situations are common; however, they are not the same as working in an agency where family treatment is the principal form of therapy or where you and the rest of the treatment team have the option of selecting family therapy because you feel it will be the most efficient and helpful intervention.

This chapter introduces some basic concepts about family therapy. It describes how to conduct a first interview with a family and provides some guidelines as to what you are looking for in assessing how a family functions and whether or not this family is suitable for family therapy. Much of what is described should be useful in understanding the dynamics of *any* family meeting, regardless of whether or not you and the treatment team necessarily see family therapy as the best—or only—intervention.

As in the chapter on interviewing an adult client, we will start by going chronologically through the experience of conducting the first interview with a family. Before we begin, though, it is necessary to set aside our previous definition of what constitutes "the client." In individual treatment you have become accustomed to assessing the symptoms and problems and strengths of one person and evaluating the impact of family relationships on that *individual.* In family therapy *the whole family* is considered the client and your focus will be on the *interactions* between and among family members.

Even the language of family therapy is different. It derives principally from "systems theory" and assumes that communication is circular: that is, every action produces a reaction; every message will produce a response. In systems theory this is known as a loop, but it might be more useful to conceptualize the whole family as a balloon: if you squeeze it one place it bulges someplace else, and that bulge constitutes a symptoma symptom which is usually the reason why the family is seeking help. The job of the family therapist is to figure out what's causing the family to feel squeezed.

In thinking about the idea of a family symptom, it is useful to remember that the symptom usually shows up in one of five places. The first possibility is in *one of the parents.* The second is in the relationship *between the parents.* The third is *between a parent and a child.* The fourth is *between children.* And the fifth is in *one of the children.*

When the symptom appears in a child, some other agency may be involved in sending him for treatment. For instance, he may be truant, or may have become involved with the courts because of some delinquent behavior, or may have been identified as at risk for substance abuse. Or the family itself may seek help, believing it is the child who "needs to change," because he is unmanageable, withdrawn, won't eat, or picks fights with his siblings. In clinical terms, this makes the child the "identified patient."

Regardless of whether the family sees its problem as only one member, when you do a family interview it is important for you to ask yourself one fundamental question: *How might this symptom, even though it appears to involve only one person, be serving the whole family?* By bearing this question in mind you will continue to address the *whole* problem and not be diverted to a consideration of only one aspect or one person's behavior.

For example, an adolescent who is truant or experimenting with drugs may appear at first to be doing these things for no other purpose than to hurt his parents and undermine their goals for him—or even his own stated goals for himself. You may eventually discover, however, that he actually knows the parents' relationship is in trouble and that he misbehaves in order to keep the family from falling apart. After all, if a child is in trouble, parents will often set aside their own differences in order to try and help.

Another way of asking the same question is to say to yourself, "What would be going on in this family if this symptom didn't exist?" In the case of the above situation, the errant child might have sensed that unless he became the focus of the stress in the family his parents would be constantly arguing or his father might simply stop coming home. So, the child's symptom *solves* the family problem. This, then, is a key concept in thinking about how families work; that is, *the symptom is often the solution*—albeit, an unhappy or dysfunctional one—to *the family's problem.*

Given this framework, let us look at the course of the first family session. In general, you will receive a phone call or a request for help from one of the parents, but that does not necessarily mean that the parents will be seeking family therapy. Therefore, you need to discuss with your supervisor ahead of time whether or not your agency has guidelines for if, and when, you invite the entire family to attend the first meeting-

---

REMEMBER TO ASK YOURSELF

- **How might this symptom be a *solution* to some other problem the family is having?**
- **What might *that* problem be?**

even though you cannot yet know whether the problem requires individual or family treatment.

If it is your agency's perspective that the whole family should be evaluated at the start, you should attempt to arrange a first interview with as many members of the family as possible. Then it is your task during the first interview, if it seems appropriate, to redefine the problem as one that affects the whole family.

Of course, such a redefinition is not possible unless you can *see* the whole family. However, if the client has not called your agency asking for family treatment, it is quite common to encounter some resistance to the idea that everyone should come for the first meeting. Pay attention to the *form* of that resistance, because it may give you your first clue as to how the family operates, and perhaps to important cultural differences about family roles.

For example, if a wife says that her husband is too busy to come in, you may have acquired useful information about who is considered responsible for taking care of the children, or some clue to a potential conflict between the husband and wife, or some information that the family is protecting the father, or any of a number of other possibilities.

Nevertheless, if your goal is to conduct a family interview, then your task is to get as many people there as possible. In fact, some family therapists would argue that you should not conduct a first interview without all members of the family present. This might be most easily accomplished by explaining that it is the policy of your agency to see all family members, including young children, for at least one interview. The reason to encourage the presence of young children is that they are often remarkably candid in comparison with older children or adults, who have already learned the family rules about what is permissible to talk about and what isn't.

Even the presence of an infant can be informative, since the birth of a new child very often affects the feelings and relationships between siblings or between mother and father. So if the parent refuses to bring a child because "he is too young" or "he won't sit still," you might also be hearing information about the family's discomfort in sharing information with children, or the special role one child may play in the family, or the possibility that it might actually be that youngest child who needs attention or help.

When you are having this conversation about who should attend the first meeting, it is important to remember that "the family" does not necessarily consist of a mother and father and children. The general rule, in inviting people to participate, is to consider everyone living in the household—be they uncles, grandparents, boyfriends, or foster children—as part of the family. Further, if it is your impression that other significant people have a critical influence on the family's behavior, you should encourage them to come even if they don't live on the premises.

It has probably begun to dawn on you that you could easily find yourself preparing for an interview with a dozen people of all ages. This prospect raises another significant difference between individual and family therapy; that is, regardless of how few people attend, if you are accustomed to seeing only one client at a time, your first family interview will almost certainly feel chaotic by comparison. The antidote to this feeling—and an important principle of family therapy—is that the therapist conducting a first family interview plays a much more active, "take-charge" role.

As we proceed through the interview, you will acquire a clearer sense of how and when to do this, but first it is important for you to arrange a space where there is room for everyone to be seated, even if that space is not ideal. It is also important for you to go out and greet the family—all of the family. The latter is emphasized because you want each family member to understand that you value his or her participation. So, you must greet everyone individually, by name, regardless of age. Once in your office, allow the family members to seat themselves in whatever positions they find comfortable. Be alert to the choices they make.

Does one person tell the others where to sit? Do mother and father sit next to each other? Does one child sit at the far edge of the group? Does a child sit between the parents? Does grandma encourage the children to sit with her? As family members settle in, they will often give you a graphic representation of which individuals are allies, who is the outsider, who is designated to protect whom, etc.

During this getting-acquainted phase of the interview, you

will also get some sense of who wanted to come to see you and who didn't. You may be surprised to discover that the child who was identified as the problem is, in fact, eager to be there. Conversely, you may discover that he is there because the family or some outside agency insisted. You may get a sense of who feels things can get better and who feels they are hopeless. But your primary task at this stage is to make the family members feel that you are interested in each of them.

At some point you will sense that the introductions are over, or someone in the family may raise the issue of why they are here. If no one does, you should help make the transition to a less social and more working relationship with a simple question, such as "What brings you here?" or "How can we be of help to you?" As with the individual, you want to hear the family's story, but that is complicated by the fact that there is more than one person present to tell it. If someone initiates the storytelling, that person is likely to be the spokesperson for the family. Very often that will be the person who made the initial contact.

If it is the father (or father-surrogate), this may give you an indication that the family is organized along hierarchical lines, with each successive person in the family having less and less authority—and that may reflect a significant ethnic or cultural value which must be respected if you are to be helpful. If it is the mother (or mother-surrogate), you may acquire some further information about gender-related family roles and the importance of matriarchy in that family or culture.

It is important to remember that eventually you need to provide everyone with an opportunity to comment on what he or she sees as the family's difficulty. In the language of family ther-

---

REMEMBER TO ASK EVERY FAMILY MEMBER

- **What he or she sees as the problem the family is having.**
- **What *effect* the problem is having on his or her life at the moment.**

apy this is known as "joining" with each of the family members. Rather than allowing one person to speak for everyone and give an extended dissertation on why they are here, you are going to turn to Alex, after his mother has said, "Mary and Alex fight all the time, and that's the problem the family has," and ask Alex what *he* sees as the problem. In so doing, you are letting everyone know that you are an information-gatherer rather than an ally of any one person in the family. Just as with the individual interview, you should think of yourself as a traveler in a foreign country, only this time there are lots more people to talk to in order to find out what the customs are.

As you are hearing each member's perception of the difficulty the family is having, you will be listening for key phrases the family uses, for central themes that get repeated, for patterns of communication. All this information is of obvious value to you in formulating an understanding of how each family member sees the problem and experiences its effects on him or her.

A less obvious but equally important aspect of this phase of the interview is that it allows the family members what might be *their* first opportunity to hear what their siblings or parents or children see as the problem. If you have begun to create a climate of concern and interested listening, the family members may feel less need to defend themselves. They will be better able to hear—and think about—what others are saying.

This kind of joining also serves the purpose of making it clear that everyone will have a chance to be heard and that, at least for the moment, you will be in charge of who talks when. This is reassuring to families who are in conflict, although they may briefly present a united front until they feel that it is safe to disagree.

Eventually, though, and sometimes in the first interview, disagreements—or even arguments—may occur as one person is giving his or her interpretation of what the problem is. Pay attention to what happens when there is a disagreement. Who does what to keep it from getting out of hand? Do the parents act in concert or do they undermine each other? Does one child misbehave to draw attention away from the conflict? Does anyone threaten or exert an unnecessary amount of force? Do the adults look to you to bring the situation under control?

If this last situation occurs—that is, the family looks to you to bring behavior under control—you should try and avoid being cast in the role of policeman unless you are concerned that someone is going to get hurt. Within reason, it is important to see how the parents manage—or don't manage—at these times. If necessary, however, you should let people know that they can *say* whatever they want here but they cannot *do* whatever they want here. You should reiterate that everyone will get a chance to speak but that they cannot all talk at once or no one will ever be heard. Then return to eliciting each family member's opinion of what the problem is.

By proceeding in this way you reassure each member that he or she will have an opportunity to speak, you discourage interruptions, and you begin to establish an understanding that each person will be treated fairly here. At this stage, you are essentially encouraging the family members to talk to you, rather than to each other, since they have probably been talking to each other for years and something in their communications is failing them.

Once you have heard each person's description of the perceived difficulty, you want to get a sense of how the family members have been handling the problem up until now. Very often a single person or behavior has been identified as the cause, and the family has expended much time and energy trying to control that person. But you are also listening for strengths in the family's problem-solving capacities and some clues as to why the problem exists in the first place, so you can couch your comments about what you are hearing in the most positive terms rather than placing blame or agreeing with the definition of one person as the problem.

For instance, an 18-year-old may complain that his parents don't allow him any freedom. He may tell you that his mother listens to his phone calls and his father makes him bring the car home at 10 o'clock, when all of his friends get to stay out until midnight.

If you are oriented toward assessing individual behavior and motivation, you may find yourself thinking that these are overprotective parents who don't understand anything about today's adolescents. At such times it is essential to remember that this is a whole organism. The parents' attitude may very well reflect real knowledge about this young man's inability to tolerate too much responsibility. Or it may demonstrate something very important about the parents' upbringing. You might discover that they both come from families in which the parents paid less attention than they should have to their children's needs. So for these two people, the definition of being good parents may revolve around keeping close track of their child. Or father might have a distant and conflicted relationship with his own father and be determined to keep his son very close, because he believes that if he doesn't his son will eventually drift away, as he did from his father.

The point is that you do not yet understand why the parents have taken what may seem, on the face of it, to be a rather extreme position. Therefore, it is important to reflect their behavior in the most positive way possible. For instance, you might say to the adolescent, "Your parents are very watchful," or "Your parents are obviously very concerned about making sure you are okay." Such a comment both reassures the parents that you are not going to attack their child-rearing philosophy and presents to the adolescent another way of understanding his parents' behavior that allows room for further exploration.

This example raises another important point about treating the whole family. Unlike individual treatment, your work is done in the here and now; that is, you are concerned with the interaction going on right at the moment. So, unlike the first interview with an individual, you might discourage any extensive history of one family member in favor of allowing more participation in discussing the current problem and the effect it is having on each person's life right now.

The exception to this, however, would be if you have reason to believe that one family member, especially the one seen as the cause of the family's problem, is facing some other serious emotional challenge, such as the recent death of a significant person, or the early stages of recovery from alcoholism, or a psychotic episode. None of these would necessarily be a reason to rule out family treatment, but they may make the identified patient more vulnerable and less able to protect himself from his family's attitudes toward him. It is part of your job in the first interview to assess whether or not family therapy might be too difficult for that family member at this time and to discuss with your supervisor and the treatment team whether it might be better to see family members in subgroups or in individual treatment.

Such exceptions aside, you are going to focus on the interactions within the family, rather than on each person's past history and individual psychodynamics. As you are doing this, however, you are going to be alert for the presence of "ghosts": the echo of other people, dead or alive, whose behavior or attitudes might be having an influence on the family right now. For instance, in the example previously mentioned concerning the 18-year-old, you might hear his mother say, *"My* mother always knew who *I* was on the phone with."* This might be an indication that someone else's attitudes and/or values are impinging on this family's relationships.

While you are listening to the various family members describe the problem, you are also getting some sense of the *context* in which the problem has arisen. You are finding out if father just lost his job, or the family has recently moved, or a member of the family has just arrived or left. All of these factors, and many others, can shift the balance in a family; exploring them can be useful in assessing how the family adapts to change. This assessment, along with your growing knowledge of how the family has coped in the past, will give you some indication of whether you are dealing with a longstanding dysfunction or a temporary roadblock that can be moved aside, enabling the family to continue to grow and change.

Another useful tool in assessing the family's flexibility is to note how the communication system works. This will become clearer in the next phase of the interview, when you encourage family members to talk to each other about the problems they are facing. You might initiate this phase by suggesting that Alex tell his sister, with whom he is always fighting, what his sister does that makes him want to hit her. If Alex starts to talk to his sister and mother interrupts, then you have some indication

---

REMEMBER TO ASK YOURSELF

- **What is the *context* in which this problem has arisen?**

that she is the "switchboard" in the family; that is, in this family people do not communicate directly with each other. Their communications go through the "switchboard," where they may be stifled, altered, or transformed into some more acceptable form.

Or father might interrupt mother, who has just interrupted Alex, and you will discover that father always has the last word, or that mother and father are in conflict about how to raise their children, or that father is allied with Alex and mother is allied with sister. Or sister may tell Alex why he does what he does, suggesting that in this family everyone "reads everyone else's mind" and that it is necessary to help family members understand that they are different people who do not always think alike.

This phase will also provide clues to another important family dynamic: how well family members can tolerate differences. If one member of the family seems to be an outsider, is that because that person disagrees with the family consensus about what the problem is? Does anyone need to smoothe over disagreements? Is there a stifling of opinions or a sense that "we don't want to air our dirty linen in public"?

This latter phenomenon may be genuine discomfort with the new experience of family therapy and will change as the family members become more accustomed to the process. Or it may suggest more complicated fears about what might be said if differing opinions are freely aired. For instance, the family may know that mother is prone to serious depressions, which she attributes to "the constant bickering." So enforced cheerfulness and a united front may be seen as necessary to keep mother from getting sick and withdrawing from them.

Or the family may have a secret. There may be sexual abuse going on; one parent and at least one child will be aware of this, but they may believe the rest of the family members are not. Or there may be a secret that the parents have agreed to keep from the children, e.g., that mother's father committed suicide. Or the secret may be far more benign, but nevertheless something that some member of this particular family believes would be devastating: for example, that mother was married before or father didn't really graduate from college.

Secrets are often a factor in dysfunctional families. They may be shared with some members and not with others, thereby creating alliances and outsiders. Some, such as incest or alcoholism, certainly are a real threat to the family's staying together. All of them give further indications of the way in which the family communicates. You must be alert to the possibility that a family secret exists but not confuse it with discretion.

Discretion is related to another important question you should be asking yourself as you listen to the family members. That is, who's in charge? The simplest way to state this is: Are the parents the parents and the children the children? Is one child paying the bills or taking a younger brother to school because father is too anxious about money or mother is afraid to leave the house? If father's mother is living with the family, does she treat her son as another child in the family or does she recognize that she is living in *his* home? Does mother share information about her sexual life with her son?

This latter example speaks to the issue of discretion and the recognition that there are appropriate boundaries between generations that ought to be observed. A family that is too rigid about these boundaries may eventually need your help in accepting the idea that the children are not likely to be devastated by the knowledge that, for example, their father did not finish college. In fact, keeping such a secret in order to protect father may actually be doing more harm to the family than sharing it would.

On the other hand, with families where generational boundaries are blurred, where intimate details are shared without discretion, your job may be to focus the parents on re-establishing some appropriate generational lines and clarifying what roles each member of the family ought to be playing. In other words, ask yourself whether this family needs your help to tell each other more or to tell each other less.

In family therapy, the final stage of the first interview is also somewhat different from that with an individual. Family therapists believe that it is important for you to "reframe" the problem, particularly if the family believes that the "problem" is one member of the family. What you are trying to do is guide the family in the direction of understanding that this is a mutual problem, a problem in the system, not with one person. In the earlier example of the 18-year-old boy, you might say, "The issue here seems to be that the three of you have very different ideas

---

REMEMBER

- **Always "reframe" the problem so no one is to blame and each person can see how it is affecting his or her life.**

---

about how much independence is good for your son. The effect of that difference is that he feels constrained and that one of you feels fearful and the other feels as if you are not being a good parent. Perhaps in our next meeting we can begin exploring some middle ground where he feels like he has some independence and you two feel less worried."

This is similar to your job in the first individual interview, in that you are trying to find a definition of the issue the client is struggling with that sounds right to the client and constitutes some agreement between you as to where you will focus your energies. It is different to the extent that your task with the family is to point out the effect the problem is having on each member and on their interactions with each other, rather than dwelling on the behavior or feelings of just one person. Implicit in that is the recommendation that the whole family continue to come in for help.

Family members may or may not agree with you. If they agree, you will make arrangements for future meetings at a time that promotes the possibility that all members of the family will be able to come. Without such a mutually convenient time, you run the risk of the family's again deciding who needs help or of only those members coming who feel it is a good idea. You need to make clear to the family that that is not helpful or productive, that even though you may meet with different combinations of family members from time to time, your contract is with the *whole* family.

If the family members disagree with your recommendation, you have that much more information about the depth of their fears about sharing information, or about what it would mean to change, or about how intensely the family feels the necessity to protect someone. You also have a dilemma.

An experienced family therapist might tell the family that she cannot be of help if the family is unwilling to be seen as a whole and make a referral to some other agency that focuses on individual treatment. However, given your limited experience and the mandate of your agency, it probably makes more sense for you to suggest that you need to think about how you could be most helpful and that you will call them in a few days. During that time you should present the case to your supervisor and the treatment team and get some guidance on what to do next.

The exception to that would be if you feel that the identified patient (or some other family member) is in danger, in which case you might arrange to see that person for an individual session where he may be able to speak more freely. This is especially important if you sense that physical or sexual abuse might be going on, or if you feel that one family member is a danger to himself or someone else.

Making such an exception puts you in the position of verifying the family's belief that only one person has a problem. You will have to make a judgment call and accept that setback for a while if the situation seems serious enough, bearing in mind that at some future point you will look for another opportunity to work with the whole family.

five

How to Conduct the First Interview with a Child

If you are like many clinicians, your first wish would be to skip this chapter altogether, either because you work in a setting where children are not seen or because you are more comfortable working with adults. Be that as it may, even if you were to confine your case load to adults, it is unlikely you could see only adults who had no children. And even if you were to succeed in doing that, it is more than unlikely that you could acquire a case load of adults who had never been children themselves!

In other words, there are circumstances under which a baseline knowledge of child development and some fundamental skills for conducting an interview with a child are called for. Let us begin by exploring some of the differences and similarities between interviewing adults and interviewing children.

First, let us agree on a working definition of a "child" for the purposes of this chapter. Although many of the premises that will be presented here are true of both younger and older children, we are going to focus on children in the age range of five to ten years old, because unlike much younger children they have language and have begun interacting with the outside world, and unlike older children and adolescents their decisions and actions are still governed primarily by their caretakers.

This last aspect raises the first significant difference between children and adults coming for therapy—that is, children are seldom voluntary clients in the traditional use of the term. They rarely have any sense on their own that they need therapy or even that such a thing as therapy exists.

Therapists, too, are often puzzled by or suspect of the notion that a child might need therapy. After all, childhood is supposed to be a time of innocence, when life is carefree. Even though our adult clients frequently describe vivid memories of the unhappiness they experienced in childhood, it is still disconcerting to think that children can experience so much pain at such a young age. However, the sad reality is that they do, that they often know they do, and that they may need your help long before they understand what it is that you do.

Most often, children will come to your attention because someone else thinks they have a problem. School guidance counselors, teachers, pediatricians, camp counselors, child welfare agencies, or clinics that see only adults may all be referral sources. Or parents themselves will become concerned about their child's mood or—more frequently—behavior.

As with all referrals, you will want to note the source, because it will be your first indication of who is worried about this child or feels the child is in trouble. If it is not the parents, then the parents may not necessarily agree that the child has a problem, and might not have sought treatment if it weren't for a threat that the child will be suspended from school or have to stay home from day camp. That is something you must keep in mind as you prepare for your initial contact with the parents, so that you do not presume that they necessarily understand how therapy works or that it might be helpful to their child.

And you will want to hold in your mind the question, "Why now?" That is, what are the current pressures or changes in the life of the child that are causing attention to be drawn to her at this moment? Is the change that has occurred a change in the child, or is it a change in the circumstances surrounding her, such as a divorce or death of a significant person? In other words, is the child exhibiting the effects of her experiences or is someone else anticipating that she will or should?

Having framed those questions for yourself, your next task will be to organize a space where you can interview a child. As you begin to do so, remember that your purpose is not to entertain the child; rather, it is, as always, to gather information that will help you to be helpful to her. Once you understand how most children of this age communicate, you will have little difficulty organizing some basic tools for gathering information.

Unlike adults, who possess experiential and cognitive tools for describing their lives mostly through words, children often act out their feelings and their fears, their worries and their understanding—or misunderstanding—of their surroundings. Their form of communication is symbolic and metaphorical. It can be elaborate and complex, filled with rich fantasies and images, or barren and terrifying. It is called play.

This notion-that play is an expression of the inner life of the child; that play is language-may seem contrary to all you have been taught about the meaning of the word "play" as an activity done *solely* for pleasure. That is a myth about play and a myth about children—that they don't have a care in their heads. Ironically, it is the exact opposite of the other prevalent myth about children-that they are really little adults.

The truth is children are neither as uncomplicated as we sometimes wish to believe nor as sophisticated as they sometimes appear to be. As children acquire language, it *seems* as if they understand not just the same words but also the same *meanings* as adults. If one stops to think, it is obvious that children cannot possibly understand the things it has taken adults a lifetime to learn; however, this is still a presumption one can easily make around children, and one that you must guard against as you begin to search with the child for the meaning of her experience as *she* understands it.

So how, you rightly wonder, can you communicate with a child if she cannot put her feelings into words? Isn't that going to make it impossible to do therapy? Not necessarily. In fact, one of the interesting paradoxes of child treatment is that, although children have a harder time formulating feelings in words, they are also less inhibited by social pressures so that in some re-

---

REMEMBER

• **Play is language.**

spects they have greater freedom than adults to express their feelings. Also, just because a child cannot formulate her experience in a neat sentence does not mean that she won't recognize how she feels if you describe it in language she can understand. And finally, you are not trying to help someone who has lived for twenty or thirty or forty years trying to accommodate herself to her unhappiness. The source of a child's unhappiness or confusion is going on right in the here and now. Your job is to create a climate in which that unhappiness or confusion can be taken seriously, clarified, and as much as possible changed by those concerned with the child so she can continue to grow and learn without interference.

Here's how you start that process. Find a quiet place where you can meet with the child with as few distractions as possible, both for the child and for you. If you are using your office, clear away things that might be of interest to a child if you don't want her to play with them. After you have become accustomed to interviewing children this will be less of an issue because you will become adept at setting reasonable, clear limits; however, initially it can be distracting for you to be worrying that the child is going to break something you treasure. Although this rarely happens, it can be a source of anxiety.

Next, provide enough chairs for the child and any other family members whose presence seems necessary. Parents may bring all the siblings to the waiting room, or an uncle who is visiting from Detroit; however, if possible, you want to have clarified with your supervisor beforehand whether the first interview

---

**THINGS TO DO *BEFORE* YOUR FIRST
INTERVIEW WITH A CHILD**

- **Arrange a suitable space and have paper and pencils available.**
- **Ask your supervisor who should be in the interview and when they should be there.**
- **Ask your supervisor what to say to the parents and to the child about confidentiality.**

should be with just the parents and the child about whom there is concern or whether other family members should be included. Make sure you have enough room in your office for everyone, or find another suitable space.

That space should have a small table where you can leave two chairs at a comfortable distance—one for you and one for the child. If you have no such table, use a corner of your desk. Once you have set that up, it would be nice if you had a few toys available.

However, there are two important words in that sentence. The first is "nice"—not necessary. The second is a "few." Remember, your purpose is not to overwhelm the child with choices but to give her tools for expressing herself. If you do have access to toys, that is where the importance of choosing only a few comes in. When you are choosing toys, think about the child's age and race and gender but don't make your decisions based solely on those criteria. Children are imaginative. They can find a way to express themselves with very few toys.

A few small figures that resemble a family are most useful. These can be human figures or animals. Perhaps add a few toy cars. Maybe a teddy bear or other stuffed toy. Maybe a board game. Any of these would be nice. None is essential. In fact, the only essential tools in a first interview with a child are some pencils with erasers and some pieces of standard size paper. If you have crayons or markers or colored paper, better yet. If you don't you can still conduct a very informative and engaging interview with a child.

So now you have everything set up and the parents and the child are out in the waiting room. As with any interview, you are now going to go out and greet each member of the family—and you are going to greet them all in the same manner. That means you are going to say hello and introduce yourself to all of them. It also means that your voice and demeanor are not going to get childish when you talk to a child. If a child talks baby talk it is significant. If a therapist talks baby talk it is inappropriate.

Your agency or supervisor may have a particular preference for the order in which you see family members, e.g., parents first without the child, child first, etc. If there are no specific recommendations, it is probably preferable to begin your interview with the parents and the child together, unless you know beforehand that some catastrophic event has occurred of which the child is unaware—e.g., a death in the family, a pronouncement that someone (possibly even the child) has a terminal illness, a rape. Under these circumstances or if the parents specifically request it, it would be best to begin the interview without the child. If you do so, however, try to provide something for the child to do in the waiting room and explain to her that you are going to meet first with her parents but that she will get a chance to come in very soon. Also, if the child is quite young, you may want to show her where your room is and what the number is on your door so she knows where to find her mommy or daddy if she needs one of them.

So you would prefer to start out with everyone together. Your second choice would be with the parents and not the child. It would be least desirable to start out by seeing the child alone. In order to appreciate why that would be so, it is necessary to pause for a moment and think about what it must be like for parents to feel—or to be told by someone else—that their child needs therapy.

When they make the decision—for whatever reason—to bring their child for treatment, virtually all parents, even the most sophisticated about therapy for themselves, may feel sadness or confusion or, most importantly, feelings that perhaps they have not done their job as well as they might have. They may be worried that their child is going to feel more understood by you than by them, or like you better, or they may believe that you are going to blame them for their child's problems. These feelings may never be put into words; however, it is essential for you to assume, in every interview with parents, that they are at risk of being made to feel inadequate or guilty or disrespected. And you must also remember that, if that happens, it is very likely that you will lose the child as a client.

Why? Because, as we said before, children of this age are not voluntary clients. They do not come for help on their own. They do not pay for their own therapy. They do not negotiate in the world on their own. They cannot, usually, get on a bus and come to your office; even if they could, if their parents didn't want them to, they almost certainly would not do so. Even if the child somehow came on her own, the therapy would probably not be of much help. So the long and the short of it is that if you have not engaged the parents or caretakers in helping a child, then the child will probably not get help.

Engaging the parents or caretakers may not be easy—not just because they may experience all the feelings described above, but also because *your* feelings toward the parents may occasionally be hostile or negative or blaming. You may even wonder how you are going to sit through an interview with some parents.

One can wish that no such feelings might ever occur. However, as is evident in Chapter Eleven on abuse and neglect, in most therapeutic settings today one cannot avoid seeing children who have sometimes been left unprotected when they shouldn't have been, or witnessed things they should not have seen, or been given responsibilities they should not have had. Under such circumstances you may feel angry at the parents or experience a powerful wish simply to rescue a child. Those feelings are not so unusual in some situations and are often understandable. However, if you cannot shed them by talking with your supervisor or find some other way to set them aside so you can make a connection with the parents, then the child is better served by your turning the case over to a colleague who can.

So, having thought that over, let us assume you have moved ahead and are preparing to see the parents and child. Before you do so, however, you want to make particular note of the child's age. The reason to do that is because, along with all the other observations you would routinely make as you initiate any first interview (unusual physical characteristics of family members, who says what to whom, tone of the communications), you will also want to ask yourself one crucial question: Does this child look and sound and act her age?

That may seem like an odd or judgmental question, but it is not. It does not necessarily mean that the child sounds younger or looks younger than she is. On the contrary, it may mean

---

ASK YOURSELF

• **Does the child look and sound and act her age?**

that the child looks or sounds or seems to behave like a much older child. In either case, it is noteworthy because children frequently demonstrate that they are in trouble by being out of developmental "sync." And your first indication of that may very well be in a child's initial demeanor.

So you want to be alert to the child's "apparent" age versus chronological age. That doesn't mean that you must know or remember from your own childhood what a five- or six- or a seven-year-old "ought to do." Be assured that you will have no difficulty recognizing the inappropriateness of a seven-year-old being the spokesperson for her mother. And you are not looking for subtleties at this stage. If a child sucks her thumb or hides behind her mother, you might not be certain if that were unusual for a six-year-old but you would almost certainly be struck by it in a ten-year-old. You also want to note whether that behavior changes over the course of the interview, as parents and child both begin to feel more comfortable. And you will especially want to note changes in behavior when the parents leave the room and you are alone with the child.

But before you are alone with the child, you are going to start the interview, if one of the family members doesn't start it for you. If it is left to you, it is most helpful to initiate the relationship in a relaxed tone with as neutral a question as possible, for example, "How can I be helpful to you?" or "So, what brings you here?" Even though these questions sound banal, their purpose is to begin defining your role—for the child, in particular— as a caring, neutral adult. You are not a teacher. You are not a parent to this child. You're a friendly grown-up who is going to stay at a respectful physical and emotional distance from a child until the child feels comfortable and safe with you. You will smile at the child; perhaps she will smile back, perhaps she won't. You will try, after some conversation with her parents, to engage her in the discussion. Perhaps she will join in and perhaps she won't.

Before that happens, however, you will begin to get the parents' or caretakers' definition of the problem. What you are likely to hear about a child in this age range is something like "she is crying all the time" or "hitting other children at school" or "not paying attention to anyone" or some other behavioral manifestation of her feelings. You will also want to get a sense of whether that definition of the problem came from someone else, and if so, whether or not the parents concur with that other person's perception. At some point, if it is indicated, you will also want to get written permission to speak with that person yourself.

While you are listening to the parents, you are hearing something also of their discomfort with the problem. Sometimes that will manifest itself in the parents' describing their own inadequacies or other distressing things going on in their lives that make raising this child difficult. Sometimes you will hear anger or frustration with the child for not trying harder or being more obedient or listening. Sometimes you will hear just plain bewilderment.

Sometimes you will hear things that you wonder if the child should be hearing: vivid details of a divorce or a murder or any number of other situations that you cannot imagine talking about with a five-year-old in the room. If you are uncomfortable, let the parent know that there will be an opportunity to discuss such details while the child is not present.

Grown-ups sometimes think that children are not listening, even when they are three feet away. Or parents feel such a sense of urgency to talk about an issue that they overlook the child's presence. At these moments, they may even be glad if you stop them from saying something which they would ordinarily not say around their child. Sometimes, though, a parent will simply go on talking about it anyway, and you will get a glimpse of the content of this child's everyday life.

While you are listening to the parent, focus part of your attention on the nonverbal communication in the room. How is the child *behaving* while the parent is describing the problem? Do the two of them make eye contact? Do they touch each other? Does the child look at you when you look at her? Does she appear not to listen? Does she fidget? Does she move closer or further away from a parent? Does the child seem afraid? Is a parent trying to describe the problem in a way that might be comforting to the child? Does the child seem comforted? Disinterested? Is she quiet or is she trying to do things to distract herself, or you, or her parents?

When the parents have given an initial description of the problem and you have noted it, take the opportunity to draw the child into the discussion. Usually the best place to start is by asking the child, in an interested, relaxed way, if she knows why mommy or daddy (or whoever) has brought her here. You are going to ask that question, knowing full well that most children don't have a clue why they are in your office.

The purpose of the question is to begin eliciting the child's understanding of why she *thinks* she has been brought to you and to get a sense of her expectations and concerns. She will probably respond in one of three ways. First, she might shrug and say she doesn't know or she forgot; at this point her parents will express some surprise, since one of them almost certainly told her *something* about the purpose of your meeting. Or she might express some belief that you are a "doctor"; you can take this opening to find out what she thinks is going to happen to her at this "doctor's office." Or she will tell you that she is here because *she* is a problem, e.g., "I was bad," or "I threw food." If a child does the latter, she may or may not also follow it with some explanation intended to ward off the feeling of responsibility, such as, "Denise sits next to me. She always gets me in trouble," or "My teacher picks on me."

Whatever the child's response is, it will certainly illustrate an important difference between children and adults: that is, children do not think causally in the sense of connecting their actions with their feelings. You may hear many explanations of why she does what she does from a child of this age, but you are unlikely to hear her say, "I hit other children because I am angry at my new stepfather," or "If my mother didn't yell at me all the time I wouldn't cry when my teacher tells me to sit down."

You, on the other hand, may arrive at such a conclusion in very short order. You may find yourself saying to yourself, "Boy, if my father spoke to me that way, I would hit other kids too," or, "I'd be depressed if I was seven years old and had so many responsibilities." It is easy at such times to identify with the child and to want to make her feel better right away. But it is important to remember that you cannot make a child feel better if you don't understand what is *really* making her feel bad in the first place.

The way her father talks to her may be secondary or irrelevant or only happen today in your office because her father is nervous or embarrassed or afraid that there is something terribly wrong with his child. Or you may discover over time that this child's responsibilities—however inappropriate you may consider them for a seven-year-old—are actually a source of great pride to her. So the first reason to ask the child why she thinks she is in your office is to begin the process of eliciting *her* feelings about herself.

The second purpose in asking for the child's understanding is because it gives you an opportunity—no matter how negatively the parents may have described the child's role in the problem—to frame for all of them the most positive possible explanation for why they are here. Generally, after you have listened to the child's explanation you will want to let her know that she is here not only because she is doing or saying things that may be upsetting to other people but also because her parents are worried about her.

This perspective is usually quite reassuring to both parents and child. For the parents, it means that you appreciate their concern for their child—even though they may be frustrated by her or not know exactly what to do to be helpful—and that you respect their good judgment in bringing her for help, even though they may still have some doubts about whether it is really necessary. For the child, it is some reassurance that her parents have not brought her to you as punishment, which many children believe regardless of what their parents tell them beforehand.

It is hoped that this reassurance will make it possible for the child, no matter how defensive she might appear to be, to acknowledge that she, too, is concerned about what is happening. This can often be accomplished by simply asking in a gentle way if she is also worried about herself. Most children of this age can understand this question, but if the child doesn't seem to, you must get into the habit of simplifying your language so that the child *can* understand.

Once asked, a child will often acknowledge that she is worried or scared or completely confused by what she is saying or doing or that she has no idea why it is that she is feeling so sad or angry. Parents are often surprised to discover that their child knows something is wrong or is feeling so helpless or bad about herself, and this realization can help create empathy and a working alliance between you and the parents so you can set about together to help their child.

Now that the child is a participant in the conversation, you can get some of the basic information from her. For example, how old she is, what school she goes to, what grade she is in, etc. You can also get more of a sense of the precipitant for the visit. For instance, what led to the suspension from school? Or when did her grandfather die? Or how did she first find out that her parents were getting a divorce? The key to this part of the interview is simply to remember that, most especially with a child, these are "who, what, when, where, how" questions—not *why* questions—and they must be phrased in simple language the child can respond to.

Once you have engaged the child in the conversation, introduce the idea that you would like to spend a little time alone with her—if that is okay with both parents and child—and that you will then meet with them together again, at which time you will answer any questions the parents might have thought of in the interim. If the parents are comfortable with your being alone with the child, ask the child if that is all right with her. If so, usher her parents out of the office.

If it is not all right with someone, take note of whom and how each responds to the idea of being separated from the other. Suggest to all of them that perhaps they will feel more comfortable in a little while about mommy or daddy leaving the room, and then proceed with the interview in the manner about to be described, pausing from time to time to ask if it would be okay now for the child to stay with you alone. Bear in mind, however, that it may take more than one interview for the child or one of the parents to tolerate being separated—regardless of whether or not you think they *should* be able to separate. This behavior may reflect precisely the kind of developmental lag that would indicate the child's need for help.

So, with or without a parent in the room, you are now going to turn your focus to the child. Pay keen attention to her tone and her gestures and her movements—especially if her parents have just left the room. Does she seem more relaxed? More tense? Does her voice get softer or louder? Does she look like she's going to cry, or does she suddenly become physically active? The reason to attend so carefully is that you are going to try and match the style and speed of her gestures and voice so that you do not overwhelm or frighten the child by your presence.

Obviously, that does not mean that you are going to shout if the child shouts or jump if she does. On the contrary, you are going to make sure you maintain your normal, steady speaking voice and a calm demeanor. But if the child speaks very softly, or doesn't speak at all, or seems timid or withdrawn, then you must go very slowly and quietly in your efforts to engage her.

In either case, however, assuming that you have cleared a space or have set up a table, move slowly and easily toward it, inviting the child to sit there with you. Make sure that the child has easy access to the pencils and paper and that your chair is sufficiently far away that she is not going to feel intruded upon or crowded.

Children have very different senses of how comfortable they feel being close to other people. Some are used to being hugged a lot; others are unaccustomed to having any adult other than their parents too near them; most have been warned to be careful of strangers. Despite the fact that you know why you are there—and that your intentions are the best—from the child's point of view you are still a stranger.

For this and many other reasons, it is best as a general rule not to touch a child unless you and your supervisor discuss a very particular circumstance under which it is indicated for therapeutic reasons. Children in hospitals and other kinds of institutional settings sometimes need physical comforting or reassurance or even restraint, when their parents are not available to them. But if you are seeing a child in an outpatient or community setting where she is brought by parents or a caretaker, you could confuse both the child and the parents' sense of your role if you initiate the action of touching a child, however casually. And you might, unintentionally, be inviting the child to touch you, which could eventually make you uncomfortable.

None of this is meant to suggest that you must recoil from a child who wants to take your hand or sit in your lap. As with all other situations with children, this one needs to be handled in a friendly, clear way. But you would certainly want to note any initiation of or persistence in this behavior by a child, since it would be somewhat unusual, particularly if the two of you have never met before.

So once you are both seated, you are going to begin, in an

informal way, a series of assessment drawings and questions. Again, you should have discussed with your supervisor whether taking notes is acceptable, or even preferable, in the first interview with a child. If it is, you should write down the answers and comments the child makes throughout the interview as close to verbatim as possible.

But remember that children are curious about lots of things, and the child may very well ask you what you are writing. If she does, tell her you are writing down what she says. If she asks why, tell her it is because you think that what she says is important, or choose some other similar response that transmits to the child that you really are interested in what she says and does.

The first thing you want to ask the child to do is to draw a picture of a person for you. Don't specify age or gender or size or anything else. You just want her to draw a person. If she asks you questions about what you want the picture to be, try and leave it as much as possible up to the child. Don't comment on the drawing if there are things missing, e.g., eyes or fingers or clothes. Your purpose here is not to get artistry or verisimilitude; it is to get the child to give you a representation of how she sees herself.

Your supervisor can assist you in interpreting the details and the meaning of this drawing, as she can with any of the other basic drawings you might ask a child to do in a first interview. These are a house, a tree, and a picture of her family. Any or all of them will give you some preliminary insight into the child's inner world and her feelings about herself, so you should discuss with your supervisor ahead of time which she finds most useful.

Most children will willingly do a drawing, although there is the occasional child who will not. For the ones who will, be encouraging and interested and try to elicit some information about who is who in the family picture if the child doesn't tell you, or who lives in the house and what it is like inside, or what the person in the person picture does. Pay attention to the spontaneity and the richness or paucity of the child's responses. If she has difficulty talking, does it seem like shyness, or difficulty in understanding what you are saying, or resentment at being asked to do something, or simply intense concentration on the task? Does she erase a lot, or use a tiny corner of the page, or cross things out because she has made a mistake?

Some of the questions may sound like they could be part of a mental status exam, and it can certainly be as useful a tool in assessing a child's functioning as it is for an adult, provided, of course, that you remember that children see the world differently. For example, the normal inner life of a young child is often filled with imaginary characters who should long ago have disappeared from an adult's thinking. There are many other differences, which you will learn as you become more comfortable with children; the point here is that you are going to continue to observe and listen and evaluate, just as you would in any other interview, even though you may feel tempted to try and engage a child by sharing activities with her, rather than encouraging *her* to do them. For example, you may find yourself trying to get her to draw by offering to draw with her.

Eventually, if you enter into a therapeutic relationship with this child, you *will* play games with her, or allow yourself to be designated as the mean teacher, or hide behind the desk, but that will be because the *child* initiates your role, sets the stage,

---

THINGS TO DO *DURING* YOUR FIRST INTERVIEW WITH A CHILD

- **Remember that it is not your purpose to entertain the child.**
- **Let *the child* establish the distance between you.**
- **Ask her to draw a person and a house, or a tree, or her family.**
- **Ask her: *If you could have three wishes, what would they be?* Explore her answers.**
- **Ask her: *If you were going on a rocket ship to the moon and there was one seat for you and one seat for someone else, whom would you take with you?* Explore her answer.**
- **Ask her: *If you could be any animal, what animal would you like to be?* Explore her answer.**

and uses you as a character in some inner drama with which she is grappling. However, in this interview you are establishing some preliminary parameters in your relationship with her that will set you apart from other relationships she has known. Even though you may eventually play games with her, you are not a playmate, so do not try and engage her by initiating play.

When she has finished her drawings, ask if she will leave them with you. If she is resistant to that idea, suggest that she make copies of them to take home with her or start a special folder with her name on it so she can see the pictures the next time she comes. If at all possible you want the drawings to remain with you so you and your supervisor can evaluate them together. If the child refuses, try and duplicate them before she leaves and make a note to yourself of the nature of the difficulty that she has in giving them up. Does she cry or get angry or withdraw?

After the drawings, you will want to proceed to some questions that will, it is hoped, illuminate for you some of the child's concerns or feelings. Your supervisor may have her own series of questions or a particular order in which she prefers to ask them. If not, the following are probably the most frequently used.

The first is: *If you could have three wishes, what would they be?* Write down the answers and, if applicable, explore each of them a little as you go. For example, the child may wish for a big room, allowing for some exploration of the crowded circumstances in which she lives. Or she may wish for a pet because pets love you, or she may wish her mommy and daddy lived together, or any of a million other possibilities. Her wishes may be unique and complicated or seemingly simple and straightforward. In either case, they will be *her* wishes, and will often provide, if not a laser beam to guide you to the source of this particular child's unhappiness, then at least the beginning of a trail of crumbs.

When you have finished with the three wishes ask the child: *If you were going on a rocket ship to the moon and there were only two seats-one for you and one for someone else-whom would you take with you?* The answer to this question will give you a glimpse into the depths of the child's feelings of attachment and tell you whom she regards as the most significant or necessary to her. You should not be surprised or comment upon her choice, particularly if it is not the person you expected it to be. Children don't always choose their mothers or fathers. Sometimes they choose a friend; in rare cases they choose to go alone. Whatever the child's choice, you want to get a sense of why she picked that person. Perhaps it is her mother because her mother could take care of her on the moon; perhaps it is her friend Billy because Billy is smarter than she is; perhaps it is her grandfather because her grandfather is dead and she misses him.

After you have explored her reasons, go on to the last question: *If you could be any animal, what animal would you like to be?* By now you probably have a sense of how you would follow up on the child's answer, so it need not be elaborated upon here.

You and the child can then move on to a discussion of whether she would like to come back to the clinic or not. This aspect of the conversation is not intended to leave the decision about therapy to the child, and most children of this age would not expect to have a decision-making role in this any more than they would in going to see a pediatrician or going to school. However, that doesn't preclude the possibility of the child's saying, "No, I don't want to come back here."

Again, this is an invitation to explore the child's concerns and to find out what might make her feel more comfortable next time. Perhaps she wants more toys to play with here or to bring a friend next time. And perhaps you *could* use more toys in your office, or it *might* eventually be useful to see this child's friend. However, you may be tempted with children to want to make them happy quickly, rather than giving yourself time to think about what the child is trying to communicate to you about herself: for example, a wish that you would give her things that her parents do not, or to be your favorite client, or to have things from you that she thinks are forbidden at home.

Whatever the meaning of the communication turns out to be, the point is that you must be cautious about making promises to children. And the one that most frequently trips therapists up is, "If I tell you something, will you promise me you won't tell anyone?"

The question of what constitutes an appropriate level of

confidentiality with a child can seem to be an extremely complicated one, and you must clarify it with your supervisor before you see a child, since it can easily come up in a first interview. For example, a parent who is unfamiliar with how therapy works might ask you to report what a child said to you while the two of you were alone. Or the parent might want to know—if you are going to continue to see the child—how you plan to share information after the sessions. Or the child might ask you to promise that you won't tell anyone what she is about to tell you, and then proceed to report that someone is hitting her with an extension cord, or selling crack, or engaging in sexual activities with her, or that the child took a knife to herself last week.

These examples may sound extreme—they may even make you so anxious that you vow you will never see a child alone but regrettably they do happen from time to time, and you must do everything necessary to protect the child, and yourself, and to meet your legal obligations as well. These issues will be taken up in more detail in Chapters Nine and Eleven, but for now a few basic guidelines may be helpful.

First, let us consider the question of how you preserve the child's confidentiality vis-à-vis her parents and still maintain a therapeutic alliance with them. Your supervisor may have some wording she prefers, but in general you can offer the parents two things: first, that you will share with them *themes* and *concerns* that seem important in their child's behavior and feelings, without actually repeating what she says; and second, that you will certainly let them know immediately if you have any indication that the child is in any way endangered, either by herself or anyone else.

These guidelines should be presented to parents in a way that indicates that this is what is most helpful to a child. Stating them is usually sufficient to reassure them that you are not interested in excluding them; that you understand and respect the fact that they are concerned about their child; that they have a right to know; and that you appreciate the fact that they have the ultimate responsibility for their child's well-being.

From the child's point of view, the question of what you are going to tell other people may come up very early; for example, she may ask you to promise not to tell something. Again, you need to verify with your supervisor her preference for handling such situations. However, if no guidelines are available, it is generally best to explain to a child that what you and she talk about is for the most part between the two of you, but that there is one major exception: If she tells you that she is being hurt by someone else, or might hurt herself, or—in rare cases—might hurt someone else.

Therapists are often concerned that spelling this out for a child may keep the child from confiding in you if she is in danger. In fact, the effect is often the opposite, since you are letting the child know that you intend to protect her from being hurt or from being so out of control that she might hurt someone else. Furthermore, as you will discover in Chapters Eight, Nine, and Eleven, there may be circumstances under which you do not have a choice as to whether you notify the authorities or the child's parents, so telling the child in advance will help shield you from the painful dilemma of feeling that you have betrayed a child's confidence.

When you have completed the interview with the child, invite the parents back in to talk with you briefly about meeting again and to raise any questions they may have. Very often, although adults coming for therapy might not ask such a question about themselves, the parents will want you to tell them right then what you think is troubling their child and how long it will take to make it go away. These questions are certainly understandable in light of the anxiety most parents feel about bringing their child for help, and you will need to explain the assessment process and perhaps let the parents know that you may not even know for a while if yours is the right setting for their child.

After that, what remains is to explicate, if you have not already done so, the role the parents will play in helping the child. Some hold the position that a child's therapy should be free of any parental involvement. Other agencies believe you cannot treat a child without the active participation of the parents or caretakers, and perhaps of the extended family as well. Some settings by definition demand that the parents must participate; others prohibit them from contributing.

Clarify this with the parents; then offer a next appointment for the child and/or the parents depending on what seems indicated. For instance, you may next need to take a developmental history on the child—which you and a parent, or both parents, would do without the child present. Or you may want the next meeting to be a full session with just the child.

Explain to the parents the importance of consistency in keeping appointments, especially for a child in treatment. Then let the child know when and for how long you will be meeting each time, and answer any questions she may have. Lastly, escort them all back to the waiting room.

Then, as always, leave yourself a few minutes to think about, and make notes of, your observations.

six

How to Take a
Developmental History

No doubt the first question that comes to mind in approaching this chapter is: What exactly is a developmental history, anyway? If you are accustomed to seeing mostly adult clients, you may even have wished for something like a developmental history on many occasions, but not known what it was called.

When you see an adult, you are often trying to imagine what his early environment—uncolored by the effects of time or loss or fear or illness or growth or hurt—was actually like. Perhaps you have even wondered from time to time what it would be like to interview others who knew the client as a child: to hear their memories and impressions of his innate temperament, or his reactions to stress, or the character of his early attachments, or his role in the family. But for the most part such opportunities do not exist in treating adults and would not necessarily be helpful to the therapy even if they did.

This is not true for children, however. The opportunity to interview one or both primary caretakers about the child's earliest environment and experience is invaluable in making a thorough and conscientious assessment. It allows the therapist not only to acquire relatively accurate historical data about the child's life, but also—just as importantly—to gain significant access to the parents' feelings about the child in a way that is not going to endanger the therapeutic alliance between parent(s) and therapist.

Perhaps you are wondering how that can happen. How can you learn about the character of the fundamental parent-child relationship at such an early stage in the therapy without the parents' feeling that you are intruding or judging their performance as parents? The answer is the same as it is for any other good assessment tool: that the process of conducting a developmental history consists of a who-what-when-where-how series of questions. It is precisely the benign, near-plodding quality of the history-taking process that will reassure parents that you are neither going to ask that they reveal too much about themselves nor are you interested in placing blame. You simply need some facts: the who-what-when-where-how. From those facts, and all the other information you acquire along the way, the why—or whys—will eventually emerge.

Therefore, you should introduce the concept of taking a developmental history as soon as possible—preferably at the end of the first interview. If a parent has a question as to whether or not this is a necessary step in helping the child, you should explain that this is something you routinely do with every parent who brings a child for therapy. You should also make it clear that it may take as long as two sessions to complete the developmental history, and that it is best done when the parent can come to see you without any children present.

The parent referred to above is usually the mother, because this chapter assumes that the person who can be most informative in the developmental history-taking is a child's mother. However, the questions can be easily adapted if your supervisor or your agency feels that mother and father should be seen together for these interviews or that mother should do one and father the next.

There are also other circumstances in which mother would not be the first or even a possible choice. For example, some children's mothers have not had contact with them since they were born, or they are unable—for physical or mental reasons—to be adequate reporters, or they are prohibited by law from being involved in their children's therapy. Obviously, in these situations you will rely on whoever has the early knowledge of the child, or observed the mother and child together, or can make records available to you. That may be the father, or a grandparent, or a foster mother, or a hospital, or the social worker in a social welfare agency.

Your first choice, however, remains the mother. You must bear in mind that mothers of small children have far more difficulty scheduling time to do things alone than clients without children, so you will have to be as flexible as possible and not necessarily expect her to be able to schedule two interviews right then. Since it is not necessary for the developmental history to be completed before you start seeing the child or the family for therapy, working around the mother's schedule should not present a major obstacle to getting help for the child.

Assuming that you have arranged to see the parent alone, what is it that you want to know, and why? Basically, most of the information you are seeking in the developmental history focuses on the period from just before the child's birth to approximately the age of five, although a few questions will be relevant to older children as well.

The reasons to focus so intently on the early period are twofold. First is that the impact of the primary environment and caretakers is likely to be virtually undiluted during this period and, although a child may garner strength from that environment at any time in his development, it is unlikely that he will ever be as vulnerable to the weaknesses of that environment or those caretakers as in the first five years.

Second is that by the time you see the child for a particular problem at the age of six or seven or eight, he may be reacting to a complex mix of recent events, constitutional factors, environmental changes, or any of a number of other combinations-in other words, a blurred superimposition of the here-and-now on the way-back-when. The developmental history allows you a view of the child's functioning *over time*. And that, in turn, will help you to assess whether what you are observing now is a temporary setback in an otherwise steady movement toward maturity or the inevitable outcome of an earlier series of emotional or physical or temperamental mishaps which must be addressed before the child can move forward in his progress.

When you begin the developmental history you should have an outline such as the one at the end of this chapter available to you. However, you should remember that it is intended as guidelines *for a conversation*, not as a series of questions that must be answered entirely and in order. In fact, much of your sense of the relationship between mother and child may actually come from the digressions, so—time permitting—you should let them happen.

A mother will often express concern, especially if she has had a number of children, that she may not remember all the details of this particular child's early history. You can reassure her that, even though things seem a bit blurry at the beginning of this process, most mothers remember anything unusual about a particular child's history, so she can relax and just do her best.

As with the information you acquire in any interview, you and your supervisor are going to think about and interpret the information in a developmental history many times over, based on increasing knowledge of the strengths and weaknesses and adaptations and innate characteristics of parents and child. Therefore, the remainder of this chapter will focus on the *general purposes* of the developmental history and a framework for focusing your thinking and attention.

As you can see from the developmental history outlined at the end of this chapter, you begin your exploration of this child's development with the physical and psychological climate in which the mother found herself when this child was conceived. Beginning with the mother's age when she became pregnant, you obtain your first indication of the level of biological risk to this infant at birth. Was the mother 14, or 40, or within three to four years in either direction? If so, you are alerted to far ends of a spectrum where a child might be born with a greater likelihood of being physically compromised in some way, whether apparent or not. You have also commenced one of the tracks you are going to follow throughout the developmental history. That is, the building up of a profile of this child's *physical* state over his lifetime to date—as seen through the eyes of his primary caretaker.

The idea of acquiring data about the child's physical wellbeing in this way may seem redundant, since we have already explored the value of a medical history and getting a report from any client's physician—especially a child's. However, the crucial aspect of exploring the child's health via the developmental history is not only to get facts but also to get *feelings* about those facts from the person whose feelings mean the most to a child. Throughout the various areas of the history-taking, this is a significant aspect to which you will be attending.

Along with the collection of data, you will be acquiring a sense of who this woman was before she became a mother. What were her experiences of relationships? How did she see herself before and during her pregnancy? How did she respond to the reality of being pregnant and to the child's birth and to the innate endowment with which this child was born? What was the social and cultural environment which surrounded her and her newborn baby? What impact did her physical and psychological state have on the child? And what impact did the child have on her physical and psychological state?

As you look over the questions at the end of the chapter you will see a steady progression of questions focused on the physical well-being first of the mother, then of the mother and child, and then of the child. Also in that first series of questions are hints of the depth of the *attachments* in this child's orbit. First you will explore the sense of connection between the two people who produced this child. Answers to the questions of how long they had known each other or whether the pregnancy was planned or unplanned are going to give you your first inkling of what these two people meant to each other and what a child produced from that union might represent. For example, a child born to a woman who had been trying unsuccessfully for many years of marriage to produce a child could result in a very different initial sense of attachment than a child borne of a casual liaison or a sexual assault.

However, one must as always proceed with caution in making assumptions, such as assuming that because a child was unplanned he was unwanted; or that a parent has been so wounded by the realities of life that she could not cherish her child; or that a parent who expresses anger or resentment toward a child does not still wish to be a good parent.

For these reasons and many others, you will explore the mother's awareness of her own *psychological* state during her pregnancy and the infant's earliest days, both directly by asking about it and indirectly by inquiring about such things as the baby's sleeping habits, which will often have a direct effect on mother's ability to feel rested and at ease.

Or perhaps you will get some sense from a response to the question about babysitters that this was a mother who found it difficult to tolerate being with her baby for long periods of time. Or the question about hospitalizations of the parent during this period in the child's life may lead to a discussion of a postpartum depression.

At the same time as you are developing an impression of the mother's psychological condition, you will also be getting information about this child's *innate temperament*. Even a simple question about the baby's sucking pattern at birth will give a clue to this particular infant's degree of physical intensity. Responses to such questions as whether or not the baby was cuddly or walked at a very early age may suggest that this was a child born with an active, restless disposition or one whose basic biological nature was more placid. This sort of information will help frame questions for you about the current problem for which this child is being brought to you and what part his inborn characteristics might be playing in that problem.

As the history progresses, you will introduce a series of questions addressing standard *developmental milestones*. These are intended to explore whether the child accomplished certain physical tasks within a period that is considered normal. It is important to note, however, that this is a *range* of time. If the child did not sit or walk or talk during that time frame, it should certainly be explored and can be extremely important in assessing whether this baby was compromised in some way. However, the developmental lag, as reported by the parent, is not necessarily diagnostic in and of itself.

For example, you may hear that this baby "took forever to say a word" or was "a scrawny little thing." If what the mother is expressing sounds intense or extreme, it is often useful to try and get some corroborating data. For example, you can ask the mother if she can remember discussing with the baby's pediatrician any concerns she had at the time about the baby's lack of verbal development or his slow growth. If such a conversation did take place, perhaps she can remember what the doctor said. This line of inquiry will help you differentiate, as best you can, this child's actual characteristics as an infant from this mother's *expectations*.

Most parents—regardless of whether their baby was born to them or adopted—form some mental image and some pre-

---

REMEMBER

- **Taking a developmental history is not just asking questions. It is listening for the parent's feelings of attachment and expectation about the child and clues to the child's innate temperament and developmental progress.**

---

conceived feelings about the baby, often long before he is born. These may be a dream that he will be a carpenter like his grandfather or a hope that he will be a girl, or tall, or the smartest child in his class.

Or the wishes may be subtler: that he will be loving to his mother like her brother who drowned when she was ten; or that he will make his father feel more manly because he can play baseball with his son. Sometimes, sadly, an expectant mother may wish for nothing more than not to be burdened with the child of *that* father; or that this baby will be so independent that mother—or father—can return to earning a living without feeling that the baby is being deprived; or some whole other set of thoughts and feelings about which you could not possibly be aware. You should train yourself to become alert to these expectations, because the discrepancy between the parents' expectations and the child's inherent character or capabilities may, in fact, be the reason they are in your office.

So as you progress through the developmental history you will begin to understand—one small anecdote at a time—how each of these elements—the physical, the psychological, the interpersonal, the innate disposition of parent and child, the level of developmental growth, and the parents' expectations—are interwoven to form the unique character of the relationship between these particular parents and this particular child. And with that will come some emerging sense of the bonds between them, and whether those bonds are strong enough to support the child through the crucial emotional, physical, and developmental tasks he must now achieve in order to move to the next level of experience and growth.

THE DEVELOPMENTAL HISTORY

Keep in mind that you will need to adapt these questions based on whom you are interviewing, as well as to cultural differences and to the economic and social conditions in the parent's life.

1. How old were you when you met your child's father?
2. How old was he?
3. How did you meet?
4. How soon after you met did you become pregnant?
5. Was the pregnancy planned?
6. Before that, had you ever had a problem getting pregnant?
7. Had you ever had a miscarriage or an abortion?
8. What was the child's father's reaction to your getting pregnant?
9. What was your family's reaction?
10. What was the father's family's reaction?
11. What was your reaction?
12. How did you feel physically during the pregnancy? Did you have regular checkups? Where there any complications?
13. How did you feel emotionally during the pregnancy?
14. Was it a full-term pregnancy?
15. Did you take any medications during the pregnancy?
16. Who went with you to the hospital when the baby was born?
17. How long were you in labor?
18. Were you given any medications during labor or delivery?
19. Were there any complications during delivery?
20. How much did the baby weigh?
21. How long did you stay in the hospital?
22. Did you and the baby leave together?
23. When you left the hospital, with whom did you go to live?
24. In the first few weeks, who helped you with the baby?
25. Who made the decision about the child's name? Who was the child named after?
26. Who does the child look like?
27. Did you breast feed or bottle feed? For how long? How was the baby weaned?
28. Did the baby have a strong sucking instinct?
29. Was the baby a good eater? Is this still true?
30. What were the baby's early sleeping habits?
31. Was the baby "cuddly"?
32. Do you think that your child began to sit, stand, walk, or talk unusually late or early? Did anyone else ever tell you that about your child?
33. When was your child toilet-trained?
34. How was your child toilet-trained? By whom?
35. Did you work during your pregnancy?
36. Did you go to work after the baby was born?
37. Who took care of the baby when you had to leave for any reason?
38. Has your child ever been ill? At what age? For how long?
39. Has your child had any serious accidents?
40. Has your child ever been hospitalized? For how long?
41. Since your child was born, have *you* ever been hospitalized? Why? For how long? Who took care of the child?

(continued)

42. Does your child have younger brothers or sisters? What was your child's reaction to their birth?
43. Has your child ever asked any questions about sex? What? How did you answer?
44. Have you ever been aware of your child masturbating? What did you tell the child?
45. What was the earliest grade your child attended in school, including nursery school? How old was your child?
46. Did your child ever have any difficulty separating from you to go to school?
47. Has your child had any learning problems in school?
48. Has your child had any behavior problems at school? Or at home?
49. Who disciplines your child, and how?
50. Does your child have friends?
51. Has your child ever slept away from home?
52. At home, does your child share a bedroom? With whom?
53. Who is the child close to in the immediate and in the extended family?
54. Has anyone who was important to the child died? Under what circumstances?
55. Has the child been separated from anyone who was important, either by that person moving or by you and the child moving?
56. Were you and the child's father married? If so, are you now divorced or separated?
57. When did the child last see his father? Under what circumstances?

seven

How to Conduct the First Interview with a Couple

There may be many occasions—especially if you treat children and families—when you will have two people in your office whom you consider a couple. They are not, however, necessarily seeking, or even suitable for, couples therapy. This chapter will be devoted to defining "a couple" for the purposes of therapy, to introducing some basic concepts of couples treatment, and to exploring how to conduct the first interview when you and your supervisor have concluded that seeing the couple together is indicated. Let us begin with two basic ideas.

First, the concept of a couple to be used in this chapter is as follows: any two people who have, or *have* had, or *wish* to have an abiding, intimate relationship. Those two people may or may not be married. They may or may not be a male and a female. They may or may not have, or have had, or wish to have a sexual relationship. They may or may not be of the same race or religion or social strata—or even of the same generation.

In other words, even though the impact of family or societal attitudes on their choice of a partner may eventually turn out to be a significant issue in the treatment of these two individuals, your initial interest, as a therapist, is in whether or not the two people who appear before you do, or ever did, consider *themselves* "a couple."

Second, "a couple" may or may not have come to see you originally for couples therapy. They may have come to you for treatment of their child, or for individual treatment, or for some other purpose entirely. In other words, they may not have initiated treatment with the idea of being seen together or because they necessarily understood that their feelings or behavior were affecting their relationship with a partner or that their relationship with a partner was affecting their feelings or behavior. Those realizations may have evolved in the course of some other kind of treatment with you or some other therapist.

On the other hand, of course, the two people you find before you may have sought you out precisely because one or both felt strongly that something in the interactions between the two of them was causing unhappiness. It is frequently the case with couples that one of the partners is experiencing this unhappiness much more keenly than the other. Consequently, you are going to begin your thinking about this couple—possibly as early as the initial phone contact with one of them—by asking yourself whether you have two "voluntary" clients asking for help or whether one of the partners may be feeling as if she is being forced into therapy by a wish to keep her partner "happy" or by an implicit threat that she will lose her partner if she does not come to see you. This difference in feelings about the need for couples therapy is not a contraindication, but it is something you should think about so that you do not presume—especially in the first interview—that both partners are willing participants.

Another tempting presumption to avoid is the notion that the couple is seeking your help in order to *continue* the relationship. Even though that may appear to be their intention—or at least the intention of the partner who calls—it may turn out that these two people are actually coming to you at a point where one or both sense—or one of them has already decided—that

---

Remember

- **Do not assume that both partners wish to stay together.**

the day-to-day relationship is ending or must end. Your help is actually needed in order for them to find a graceful, fair, or comfortable way to make this ending.

It can be quite difficult for a therapist to avoid becoming invested in seeing a couple stay together, particularly if the partners are elderly, or there are children involved, or one partner will suffer severe economic hardship if the other partner leaves. However, it is especially important at such times to remember that one cannot be of help if one cannot "start where the clients are." If the idea that you may ultimately be a compassionate overseer of a relationship's demise is not one you feel comfortable with, then perhaps you should decline the case.

These are all issues that will require some thought before you see the couple. If you have the information available to you after the initial phone contact, you might also want to start thinking about the life stage that each of the partners is likely to be in, as well as the probable stage of the relationship. For example, you receive an application from a married couple seeking therapy. The wife is 32 years old and from the application you can see that she has three children: a 14-year-old girl and a ten-year-old boy by a previous relationship, and a six-month-old baby by her present husband, who is 26 years old.

Even with this minimum amount of information, one might consider that this is a woman whose late adolescence and early adulthood—a time she may have seen others devoting to "sowing their wild oats"—were spent taking care of two babies, with or without a partner to help share in the responsibilities. On the other hand, her new husband appears to have had almost eight more years than she to complete the emotional tasks of growing up before he had a child himself.

These differences in opportunity to complete stages in their personal development may have important ramifications in their relationship and their expectations for one another. For instance, the wife in this example might see marrying a younger man as a way to recapture some time she felt was lost by having babies at such a young age, while he might have chosen her because he saw her as more experienced and stable—a woman who would help him "settle down" if he was having difficulty doing so on his own.

Such divergent styles of addressing issues of personal

growth are not at all unusual and may be perfectly appropriate to the stage in which the individual partners find themselves. However, they have the potential to cause considerable strain in the relationship if the expectations that accompany them are at great variance with each other. In any case, however, they certainly require attention and evaluation on your part if you are going to be helpful to the couple.

You must also give some thought to the stage of the relationship itself. Using this same couple as an example: They are probably relatively recently married and are certainly new parents. However, if they are indeed newlyweds, they are newlyweds who found themselves with two children on the day they got married, perhaps interfering for both of them with the opportunity to be alone, to get to know each other as a married couple, and to work out some of the stresses that inevitably follow on the heels of any momentous life decision. Further, perhaps not long after they were married, they had a baby, which for one of them was an entirely new experience. He was catapulted, for the first time, into parenthood, while his wife had experienced this twice before.

Here, too, it is not hard to imagine ways in which such a move to a different phase of the relationship could be disruptive. With this same couple, for example, the wife may have hoped—after such a long period of being solely responsible for a family—to have a time of feeling taken care of herself before resuming the role of nurturer; meanwhile, the husband may have married when he did—and perhaps whom he did—not only because he wanted a wife but also because he wanted a child. In part, he may have chosen this particular woman because she had already demonstrated her capacity to be a good mother.

ASK YOURSELF

- **What life stage is each of the partners in?**
- **What life stage is the relationship in?**
- **How does this couple manage the issues of inclusion, control, and affection?**

Again, these are not necessarily conditions that insure that a relationship will suffer, and you should not presume that you understand, before you even see two people, more than they do about what has been helpful or harmful in the choices they have made. But you should be alert to, and think ahead about, what such circumstances might do to the hopes and expectations each had for herself and her partner when they entered into the marriage. In so doing you begin preparing yourself to answer the question that should always be in your mind as you ready yourself for a first interview of any kind: that is, why now?

Having thought about all that, when the couple actually arrives in your office you will harken back to many of the principles you used for commencing a family interview. There will be introductions, some brief casual conversation, some mental notes to yourself about where the partners seat themselves, any noticeable physical characteristics, unusual speech or thought patterns, etc. And you will remind yourself about the importance of joining with both partners in identifying their concerns. After these amenities and observations, you begin the actual interview by asking each of them what *he* or *she* thinks the problem is between them.

The answers to this question are of obvious use to you as the therapist, and you should write them down and briefly explore their meaning to the partner who is describing her impressions. However, there are other important reasons to start the interview with this question. One is that this may be the first time each of the partners has actually articulated a perspective on what the difficulty is that the two of them are having. Later on you will want to ask both partners whether or not they were aware that this is how their mate saw the issues between them. Very often, the answer is no. One partner frequently will express surprise and, under the best of circumstances, some interest in or curiosity about the description of the problem.

The other reason to start with this question is to discover whether or not these two people can tolerate listening to each other's point of view at all, and if not, what they do to avoid it. There are many different ways in which one partner can communicate to the other—or to you—that she disagrees with, or does not believe, or simply has no interest in hearing what her partner is saying. These communications can be quiet and subtle:

for example, turning away, or becoming sullen or withdrawn, or simply not responding, or, when it is her turn to speak, just moving on as if her partner had said nothing. Or, they can be vocal and obvious. For example, one partner may interrupt the other, or talk over her, or talk louder, or talk directly to you while the other partner is responding to your question. Or one partner may begin to make nonverbal "comments" to distract you from what the other is saying or small asides intended to devalue the content of her partner's grievances. Or the two of them may simply start to argue as if you weren't in the room. Or, regrettably, one partner may menace the other physically or verbally in order to stop the discussion.

Assessing the seriousness of a threat of physical harm will be discussed in detail in the next chapter. Let us first address the more benign—but often equally unproductive—ways in which couples sometimes interact. A therapist doing couples work, especially for the first time, can find it particularly difficult to feel that she can be helpful to two people when they can't even tolerate differences of opinion about the nature of the problem. And when they start off by raising their voices or being verbally abusive to each other, it is particularly hard to think of a useful way to intervene.

So, how are you to think of this behavior in a way that will allow you to make good use of it? Well, perhaps the most constructive way to conceptualize what you are witnessing is to think of it as a home movie. These two people are allowing you to see for yourself—and assess for yourself—how they interact with each other right now. You are not hearing a polite, cautiously edited report of a disagreement that occurred yesterday, or last week, or five years ago; you are watching the relationship as it is at this moment in time. And the more uncensored the interactions are, the more of a feel you are going to have of how each of them handles conflict and of what they need from you.

So you should let them argue for a few minutes. Then you should stop them. Ask them if this is how most of their disagreements go. The answer is likely to be yes. If that is the case, then you should thank them for letting you see what *isn't* working. You should tell them that this has been very helpful to you, but that it is probably not very helpful to them. The three of you need to establish some understanding about, and guidelines for, talking that will make it possible for each to express an opinion in a way that insures that he or she can speak without interruption and at least *allows* for the possibility that the partner will listen and eventually respond.

However, before we go on to setting these guidelines, it is important to emphasize that disagreements—or even arguments—are not *necessarily* something to be discouraged in treating a couple. In fact, as you make your assessment of a particular couple's interactions, you may notice that they never really express any disagreement and that one—or both—are quick to draw back if they happen to approach any genuine source of conflict.

Therefore, it is extremely important for you to make a distinction between constructive and destructive arguing. You must assess whether the way in which this couple agrees—or disagrees—produces useful changes in their relationship and leads to growth and a better understanding between the two of them, or whether they are on "spin cycle"—just going around and around on the same issues rather than moving on to a new level of mutuality.

One of the reasons this aspect of the assessment can be so difficult for the therapist is that you yourself may find rageful silences or cursing or yelling extremely unpleasant and discomfiting. Or your own cultural background may be one in which disagreements are to be mollified or subdued as quickly as possible.

With such feelings and experiences in your own life, it is hard to think that these two people might actually find such behavior quite familiar and comfortable and in no way a deterrent to a useful resolution of their differences. If so, it is you who may have to adjust—at least for a while—to a higher decibel level than you are accustomed to, or sulking silences, or some linguistic indelicacies.

However, if the major purpose of one or both partners' communications is to try and make the other person feel to blame for *all* the problems in the relationship, then you should gently introduce the notion that, by definition, in a relationship both partners bear an equal responsibility for the conflicts they are having. Suggest that they do something as pragmatic as trying to start their sentences with "I" rather than "you" for a while, that they try to focus on what they are each *feeling* rather than on what their partner is *doing*.

But if the problem in the interaction is the threat of physical violence by one partner against the other, then a rapid intervention is called for. Again, this can be extremely disconcerting to you as the therapist, especially if you have any sense that some of that threatening behavior could eventually be aimed at you. This subject is discussed at length in the next chapter, along with guidelines for managing your anxieties. Let us focus here on threats by one partner against the other.

It is extremely difficult at such times not to identify with the threatened partner and not to rapidly lapse into moral rhetoric about individual rights and respecting the sovereignty of others, etc. And all of those comments may be entirely correct and decent. However, they are frequently ineffective in stopping the behavior. Why? Because they can easily give the impression that you have just "taken sides" or become frightened yourself, either of which would probably preclude the aggressive partner's seeing you any longer as a fair and impartial and effective listener.

What is probably more useful is to explain that there is really no way in which you can be useful as a therapist—or proceed with the interview—if someone is in danger of being hurt. Then you can inquire whether the threatening partner feels she can control her behavior so the session can continue, or whether she would prefer to step outside for a few minutes, or whether she would rather come back next week when she is feeling calmer.

Depending on her response, you can make a simple contract about other ways she can signal that she is losing patience with her partner. Then you can proceed with the interview. However, whether or not—or how—one conducts therapy with a couple where there has been or might be assaultive behavior is a complicated and frequently controversial question. You will certainly want to explore the agency's policies about such behavior as well as discuss with your supervisor, before the next session, how to address threats of, or actual physical aggression by one or both of the partners which may be happening when they are *not* in your office.

So, let us assume that the interview is going to continue with a contentious couple or a pair who talk "at" each other. The first guideline to establish is that for now they will each talk *to you* during the session rather than trying to talk to each other, and that each partner will agree to let the other finish a thought so that you can get some of the basic information you need in order to better understand their differences. This agreement will allow you to ask questions and get answers without either of them feeling quite so defensive, and should facilitate a freer flow of conversation.

In addition, when such guidelines are introduced—in *any* initial interview in which structure-setting is needed—it also serves another extremely important purpose: It suggests that you might know some things that can be helpful to these partners in changing their behavior.

This is not to say that you know everything, and that if they simply sit back you will be magically able to fix their problem. What it can do, though, is to introduce some optimism into the process, because when two people have been struggling for a long time with the same failed communications it is terribly hard to sustain any hope that things might change for the better. And without hope, the effort of therapy will seem enormous.

Even when you do not need limit-setting in order to do so, you can remind a couple of better times by proceeding to the next stage of the interview, in which you get some brief history of *the relationship*. Especially when you are used to seeing only individual clients, it can take some practice to accustom yourself to the idea that in seeing two people as a couple the purpose, especially in the first interview, is to find out about these two people *as they are related to each other*. You will, nevertheless, note significant characteristics or historical infor-

---

ASK BOTH PARTNERS

- **How they met.**
- **What attracted them to the other.**
- **Whether they wish to work on improving the relationship.**

mation about each of them as individuals that you believe will eventually be relevant to current issues in their relationship.

First, though, inquire about the circumstances under which they met. As with all history-taking, their answers to this question will provoke many others, such as: How old was each partner? Was this the first serious relationship for both of them? How did each of their families feel about their choice of the other person? etc. If any or all of the answers emerge in the course of their recounting of their earliest relationship, so much the better. If they don't, it is preferable at this point to set those questions aside and allow the couple to reminisce for a while about a time when things in the relationship felt differently from now. You should use this as an opportunity to point out those things that sound as if they were meaningful, positive connections, even if you all have a sense that this relationship is coming to an end in its present form.

Why would you want to do such a thing at this moment? Because if the couple is going to work on the relationship, they need to be reminded that times *were* better once, that there is some foundation on which this partnership was built, and that, with some help from you and effort on their part, perhaps they can recapture some of those feelings and reconstruct those building blocks.

If this relationship is actually beginning to come to its end, then the retelling might begin the subtle process for both of them of realizing that those early feelings were a long time ago and can never be recaptured. You may or may not necessarily be aware that this process is occurring, but *they* may experience some beginning acknowledgement that there is a real ending commencing to a relationship that has had a history over time and a life of its own. Without such a realization and an acceptance that they must face this ending and mourn the loss of this relationship—whether together or separately—their ability to move forward and grow as individuals will be slowed or perhaps permanently compromised.

In either case, once they have finished describing their first meeting, you will want to know from each of them what it was that attracted them to the other. Once again, these are crucial responses that you should explore fully. Try to get each partner to elaborate. You should write down the responses as close to verbatim as possible, because contained in these answers will be some sense of what each hoped to find in a mate and whether it might be the absence—or presence—of those qualities that is now causing disappointment or friction.

That may sound like a paradox: that it could be either the absence *or* the presence of the very qualities each saw in the other that is causing conflict. It is, in fact, less puzzling than it sounds. Some examples will perhaps be helpful, but only in tandem with an understanding of each of three basic issues that a couple must resolve early in their relationship in order for it to grow without dissension.

The first essential issue partners face when they become a couple is the question of *who is going to be included* in their life together and who is not. For example, one partner may tell you that she was originally attracted to the other because the other had so many friends, or such a wonderful family, or seemed so at ease with new situations. And that may, indeed, have been the *appearance* her prospective mate presented. Or it may have been exactly what the partner *thought* at the time that she wanted for herself—to be a part of that warm, loving family or have all those caring friends.

However, the reality of the relationship over time may have proven something quite the contrary. Perhaps she found that her mate's family commitments took too much time away from their relationship, or that having so many casual acquaintances did not gratify her wish for a few close friends, or that being close to one's family meant that family members would come to live with you when they could no longer live by themselves and that she deeply resented their intrusion into her privacy.

Or perhaps her need for all that warmth and intimacy with all those new people really did remain *exactly* as it had been when the two were courting. It could be the case that during that period of assessing each other as prospective partners her mate was actually choosing her because she seemed independent, made few demands on others, and had such an admirable ability to keep other people from intruding into her life.

It is not hard to see, in this example or many others you can no doubt conjure, how two people could start off by misinterpreting a quality they see in the other as being valuable, because it is so different from their own disposition. However, it is also not hard to see how, with an issue as fundamental as who will be in their life and who won't and to what extent, the impact of those differences might have a profound effect on their relationship.

Whenever there are differences—and there must be *some* in any relationship between two people—then the second fundamental question that must be addressed in order for a union to endure is: *Who has control,* and over what? To say that this issue can present itself in a thousand guises is still to underestimate what a formidable force it can be in any relationship.

Once again, this could have been a principal aspect of the initial attraction between two people, and a factor dangerously undermining their relationship today. For example, a partner may tell you that the attachment was based in some measure on feelings that the other person seemed to know what needed to be done and did it, or never seemed to get uptight about money, or seemed completely comfortable with the idea that both would pursue their careers without interference. However, that same partner who saw all that in her mate back then may report that she now finds the other one too domineering, or unwilling to allow her to share in financial decisions, or critical of the fact that she has just taken a job that will require her to travel.

Given such scenarios, you might be able to see how unresolved issues involving control and choice-making are coming into play in the couple's current problem. Or one can certainly imagine the potential necessity to renegotiate this aspect of a relationship if a dramatic change occurs in the balance of control between two partners such as might take place if one of them developed a debilitating disease or suffered a job loss. In addition to these more apparent examples, however, this aspect of conflict resolution can be significantly more difficult and infinitely more complex when it involves subtler issues such as emotional control, or when children are used as intermediaries, or when financial or physical control resides predominantly with one of the partners.

So you will be listening for this theme in the description of each partner's attraction to, and problems with, the other oneas well as conflicts involving inclusion and exclusion of others in their life. And you will also be attentive to signs of the third major area that couples must negotiate for a successful outcome: *affection*. How close or how distant does each of these partners need to be to the other in order to feel safe or comfortable or cared for or loved? Is there a significant difference between the needs of each partner in this regard? Does one express a wish for the other to be more demonstrative, while the mate complains of feeling smothered or intruded upon or of constantly having to perform?

After the partners have finished describing how they met and what attracted each to the other, you will want, if you have time, to explore some brief history of the family configuration from which each of them came. Pay particular attention as you go to any suggestion either makes that the other reminds her of her mother, or her father, or any other significant person from her past. If such a reference is made, you will certainly want to know in what way her mate and that person are similar; make note of it and discuss it with your supervisor.

And finally, if there is time, you may or may not wish to take the opportunity, again briefly, to explore something about the level of intimacy they are currently able to achieve. "May or may not" refers to the fact that some therapists feel this is too intrusive a subject to raise in a first interview, while others contend that it is important to include intimacy and sexuality as appropriate subjects of discussion in couples therapy from the outset. Often, unless the therapist brings up these topics, they are never raised.

If you and your supervisor concur in this view, then you should ask the partners if their level of intimacy has changed in the course of their relationship. If so, in what way? For example, are they currently having a sexual relationship? If not, when and why did it stop? If so, is the frequency satisfactory to both of them? Has anything changed about their level of desire or arousal? Are they both orgasmic? If not, were they ever?

Clearly, however, this and many other questions you might raise in the first interview with a couple are predicated on the assumption that the partners wish to try and work out their differences and stay together-an assumption, as suggested before, which may not be true for both partners. Although it is impossible to say *where* in a first interview you would ask the question, *Do you want to work on improving your relationship?* it is certainly important, before you bring the interview to a close, that you *do* ask it directly of each partner.

If the answer on the part of both clients is yes, then you can move toward the end of the interview with a discussion of such issues as scheduling and fees. If one partner has expressed uncertainty, then it is time to explore how the couple wishes to proceed with this process—if at all.

Do they want to think it over, or talk it over, and get back to you? Or has it become clear in this brief process of exploration that they now need to speak next to their pastor, or children, or lawyers, or friends? Once those questions are resolved, you will have completed your first interview with a couple.

eight

HOW TO DETERMINE WHETHER A CLIENT MIGHT HURT SOMEBODY—INCLUDING YOU

In the last chapter the question of menacing or disruptive behavior was raised in the context of one partner of a couple threatening another. In this chapter we will explore how to think about, how to find out about, and what to do about the possibility that a client might present a potential threat to somebody else—including you. These concepts apply whether the client is seen in an inpatient or outpatient setting and whether he is seen with others or by himself.

If the notion that a client might represent a threat to you seems hard to think about, then it is important to pause for a moment and do a little purposeful stereotyping—this time about ourselves.

Therapists tend, very often, to devote a great deal of their mental and physical energies to the needs of others. We are seen by the world, and frequently by ourselves, as sometimes thinking more about the difficulties our clients are experiencing, their need for human contact and acceptability and reassurance, than about our own needs. And because we frequently work with people who have dread diseases, or are thought of by the larger community as "misfits" of one stripe or another, or are seriously mentally ill, or have committed heinous crimes, we are regarded as being "gutsy" or "noble" or "fearless." Unfortunately, sometimes we believe everything we hear about ourselves.

If that remark sounds critical, it is not meant to be. It is intended to alert you to the possibility that one of your greatest virtues as a therapist—your concern for the other person's feelings—might sometimes put you in jeopardy. It may be more difficult for you to allow yourself to recognize when you are in danger than it might be for someone who isn't as concerned about others. Further, if you believe that you are always supposed to appear "gutsy" or "noble" or "fearless," and that anything less is unprofessional, you might ignore some healthy, appropriate signals from yourself that you are at risk.

It is hoped that, if this book does nothing else, it will succeed in transmitting to you that there is absolutely nothing unprofessional about doing everything you can to appropriately safeguard your physical and mental well-being. In practical terms, that means that if you are afraid, you should tell someone. If you need information, or reassurance, or a second opinion, you should ask. And if you don't feel more secure, you should ask again.

Furthermore, if you are newly arrived in an agency, there should be procedures already in place for managing client's behavior and for minimizing the danger to the staff. Depending on the setting in which you work, these can include an inter-office buzzer system, a code word for alerting other staff that you are at risk, even a manual on ensuring worker safety. Ask your supervisor to sit down with you and go over these procedures in detail. Ask questions. Find out the chain of command in the event that you need to have assistance. Speak to your coworkers about what they have done in the past. In other words, take every opportunity to familiarize yourself with the procedures. Then think about them; don't assume that someone else is necessarily thinking about them for you.

When you are fully satisfied that you understand all the guidelines and procedures for protecting yourself, find out everything you need to know about your responsibilities and legal obligations in the event that a client talks about hurting a *specific* other person while in a session with you. Again, ask all the questions you need to ask. For example, to whom should you report such comments? What, if anything, should you say to the client? What, if anything, should you say to the person who was threatened?

REMEMBER

- **Find out what your legal obligations are if a client tells you he is going to hurt a specific person.**

Having done all that, you are ready to add to your array of assessment tools some guidelines for thinking about a client's potential for violent behavior, starting with two general principles. First, a client who has been violent in the past has not necessarily been violent in a way that is dangerous to you as a therapist. Therefore, you have a particular responsibility to him-and to yourself—to make as thorough an assessment as possible of this aspect of his conduct. Otherwise, you may feel unduly fearful of that client or think that he should not be offered services at your agency. Second, a client who has *never* exhibited violent behavior before may have reached a crisis point where his impulse control is threatening to fail him. So, regardless of whether you are conducting a first interview or the person has been known to your agency in some context for years, you should be alert for both visible and historical signs of potential violence.

We will start with identifying the historical signs. In order to do that, we begin where we always begin: by using what we know before we meet the client. If there is a case record, read it carefully, this time looking for some specific features, the first of which should be the client's *diagnosis*—although it is important to state at the outset that, regardless of how benign the diagnosis may be, it is never a guarantee that a client won't commit a violent act. However, along with many other factors you will explore in reading the case record, it may help you to evaluate his dangerousness to *you*.

Knowing the diagnosis may be helpful to you in your preliminary thinking about this client, because some disorders have impulsivity or loss of control of aggressive feelings as a criterion. If you have not done so before, you should find a current edition of the *Diagnostic and Statistical Manual of Mental Disorders* (DSM) or some other diagnostic manual your agency

---

**WHAT TO LOOK FOR IN THE CASE
RECORD WHEN ASSESSING A CLIENT'S
POTENTIAL FOR VIOLENT BEHAVIOR**

- **A diagnosis that includes violent or impulsive behavior among its criteria**
- **A previous history of violent behavior**
- **A history of substance abuse**
- **An injury to the head**
- **An injury to the central nervous system**
- **A previous history of physical abuse by others**
- **A previous history of suicidal behavior**
- **A previous history of delusions or hallucinations- particularly command hallucinations**

---

prefers, and familiarize yourself with the criteria for the diagnosis of this client.

At the same time, however, you should bear in mind that what appears in the case record is someone else's diagnosis of this client. You need to evaluate that source for reliability and recentness of the diagnosis. Further, as you already know, you can never, in any assessment, make your judgment about a client based on only one factor. However, if the criteria for the diagnosis this client has been given does include a potential for violent behavior, you should be certain to include that information in your discussions with your supervisor before you meet the client.

The next aspect of the case record on which you should focus your attention is the client's previous *mental status exam*. By now it is hoped that you have had an opportunity both to do a mental status exam on a client and to discuss it with other team members, so that you have had some experience with the various definitions and categories. If not, you are looking particularly for indications that this person exhibits a high degree of suspiciousness, or impaired judgment in social relationships, or a preoccupation with violent thoughts, or a history of delusions or hallucinations—particularly command hallucinations ordering him to hurt himself or someone else. When you are ready to discuss this case, these facts from the mental status exam should also be shared with your supervisor.

The next thing to look for in this client's case record whether it is called a biopsychosocial assessment, or a comprehensive assessment, or a diagnostic evaluation, or any other name—is a written history on this client. First take note of how old the document is. The reason for this is that, in evaluating a client's potential for violence today, you are interested in some perspective over time on his judgment, impulse control, and most importantly, *previous violent behavior.*

Pay attention to *how long* this person has been acting in an impulsive, unpredictable, or assaultive way. For example, was he frequently suspended from school for fighting? Was he considered a delinquent by the juvenile justice system? Was he thrown out of his parents' house for starting trouble?

Next you want to know, when he did start trouble, *how serious* did it get? Did he use a weapon, or send someone else to the hospital, or did he punch his fist through a wall?

And *how often* has he been involved in violent behavior? Does the history, for example, suggest numerous arrests on minor charges that involved brawling or gang fights? Or did he hurt only one person on one occasion? If so, who was that person, and how did the incident start? Is the prospective client a person who hit only his girlfriend? Or did he have constant verbal confrontations with his boss that eventually led to a violent outburst? Or did he never behave in an aggressive way until he was hospitalized last year?

And lastly, you are going to pay particular attention to *how recently* this client was involved in an act that was dangerous or hurtful to another person, how severe the injuries were, and whether or not a weapon of any kind was involved. If no weapon was used, did the client do sufficient harm without a weapon to require a trip to the emergency room? Or did he do something more benign, involving verbal threats or destruction of something the other person valued?

The answers to all these questions will help you and your supervisor talk in an informed way about whether or not this is an appropriate client for your agency. If he is an appropriate client for your agency, is he an appropriate client for you, based on your level of clinical experience?

However, before making either of those decisions, you need to explore a few more areas in order to have a complete profile of a client's susceptibility to violent outbursts. For example, you should also look for indications that the client has a history of *substance abuse*. If so, you should not assume—just because the client appears on paper not to have been a user for some time, or because you are meeting him in a confined setting where it is presumed that he could not have access to drugs—that he is not presently abusing some substance or suffering from symptoms of withdrawal. If either might be the case, you should remember that both current use of and withdrawal from substances that cause intoxication of any sort—be it from snorting or shooting up, getting "loaded" with the boys or free-basing—show a significant correlation with aggressive, unpredictable behavior.

Next turn your attention to the client's *medical history*, looking for several elements. First, is there any diagnosis or symptoms of *an injury to the head?* For example, has the client ever complained of persistent headaches or had seizures or a brain tumor? Has he suffered any insult to his *central nervous system*, such as Alzheimer's, or a stroke, or any other infection or exposure to a toxic substance that could cause damage? Is there any indication of *physical abuse or neglect* in his medical history? For example, does it describe bruises, broken limbs, or hospitalizations at a very young age? Or did he have an "accident" under circumstances that suggest that it might have been caused by someone else?

This last issue, past physical abuse or neglect, is something you may only be able to deduce from the medical history. It is important to evaluate, however, because its relevance for a client's potential for violent behavior may go far beyond considerations about whether or not it has caused permanent damage to the physical organism. It can also have profound implications for the person's judgment about how conflicts get resolved, or what the nature or purpose of relationships is, or how one must act to be respected in the world. Impairment in the understanding of any of these could be a factor in violent behavior.

The last piece of information for which you should scrutinize the medical history, if it is not mentioned elsewhere, is any indication of *suicidal behavior.* Were some of those "accidents" alluded to above really suicide attempts? Were injuries or hospitalizations sufficiently unexplained, or illogical, or unlikely to have been randomly caused to suggest that this client might have been intending to hurt himself? If your suspicions are raised, note your concerns and talk about them with your supervisor. Bear in mind that a suicide attempt is sometimes an impulsive, unplanned behavior, which is why it is relevant to consider as a predictor of possible violence against others.

Having explored all these areas prior to seeing your client, you and your supervisor now can make an informed decision about whether or not you will see this client. If so, you will proceed to discuss how, where, and under what circumstances to conduct the interview.

However, all that is based on several assumptions, any one of which might not be true. It presumes that you have a written record to evaluate, that your agency setting is one in which an unknown client could never simply appear in the waiting room requiring attention, and that you always have a supervisor readily available with whom to discuss your actions and decisions ahead of time.

Since none of the above may be true, let us explore how to meet a client under less desirable circumstances and still feel reasonably confident that you know how to do a preliminary assessment for the risk of imminent violent behavior. This preliminary assessment is designed to permit you to be appropriately cautious and still be calm and responsive to a client who, regardless of his presentation of himself as potentially menacing, is nevertheless a person in need of help.

In order to do that, we will spend the rest of this chapter outlining the steps you should take if one day, a receptionist or another clinician buzzes you on the intercom and tells you that there is a client waiting in the reception area about whom nothing is known, and that no one else has time to see him.

The first question you are going to ask the person at the other end of the intercom, if he or she does not offer some information, is: How does he look? If the response is, "He's pacing all over the waiting room," or "He looks stoned to me," or "crazy," or "nervous," or "loud," or "out of it," or "He sounds weird," or "He's rambling," then pursue this line of questioning

---

**EIGHT WAYS TO AVOID GETTING HURT
BY A CLIENT**

1. Know the security procedures in your agency.
2. Make appointments with new clients at times when senior staff members are in the office.
3. If the person *has* no appointment, ask the receptionist how he looks and is behaving in the waiting room.
4. When you approach a client about whom there is concern, always keep your distance.
5. Keep your hands visible throughout the interview.
6. Don't make any abrupt movements.
7. Don't sit or stand in a place that blocks his exit or yours.
8. Don't make provocative comments.

---

and get some sense of whether or not you want to alert someone else that you are concerned even before you go out to the waiting room.

Once you have made a decision in that regard, proceed to the waiting room and take a look at the client yourself. Is he staring at the floor or out into space, apparently unaware of the environment? Is he pacing or jabbering to others in an animated or agitated way? Is he looking around nervously or wiping his palms on his pant legs? Is he breathing heavily or saying scary things to people? Does any behavior or gesture suggest to you that he has a weapon? All of these are signals that will help you decide whether or not to approach the client at all, and if so, with what degree of caution.

If your decision is to approach him, your purpose is to transmit a sense of calmness but not vulnerability. You should move toward him with a relaxed gait and your hands at your sides in a casual way. You want him to be able to see clearly from a distance that you are not coming toward him in a threatening fashion. You should keep your hands visible throughout the time you are speaking with him.

As you get closer you will again be observing for certain

cues. Are the client's eyes bloodshot or bleary, suggesting substance use? Is he constantly scanning the room for indications of danger to himself? Does he look disorganized or disheveled? Does he smell?

Regardless of what you observe, you should always stop and speak politely to him from a position that assures three things: first, that you are at a sufficient distance so that he knows you cannot physically touch him; second, that you are not standing in a place—should he move toward you—from which you cannot easily step aside or retreat; and third, that you are not standing in a place that blocks his access to a doorway, should he feel the need to flee.

When you speak to this client, you should do so with the same respect you would show for any other and in a reassuring and calm way. And if anything he says or has done up to this point raises serious concern or suggests that he looks or feels out of control—or has the potential to become so—then you should find a way to conduct the initial stages of the interview standing in a place in the waiting area where others can see the two of you, but which allows the client to speak to you without being overheard.

Considering that this is your first interview with a client who has aroused some concern in you about the possibility that your own safety might be threatened, then perhaps this ought to be a prearranged signal. That is, if you make a decision not to take this client into your office, it means you would like some assistance from this point forward.

Such an arrangement would give you the experience of observing an interview with this client by a more experienced clinician. Ideally, that other interviewer should be your supervisor, but if that is not possible, then some other senior staff person should join you so that the two of you can later assess your concerns and your responses to this client. Once you have done so, it is likely that the next time such a situation occurs, you will have more confidence and certainty about how to proceed beyond this point.

So that is how you would handle the situation of a possibly violent client if you either have the option of preparing yourself ahead of time by reading data about him in his case record or have the chance to observe and assess the client in a public area. It is hoped that both of those opportunities would be used by you to prevent, if it is at all possible, a scenario in which you find yourself in your office with a client whom you begin to sense might be dangerous. Even then, it is possible to minimize the risk by keeping the door to your office open or, if it is already closed, by always sitting in a place in your office where you do not need to pass the client to open the door, preferably with a desk or table between you. Further, you can assure that your office does not contain objects that are large enough or heavy enough to be harmful if thrown.

In addition, you can talk with your supervisor about the variety of verbal methods that are helpful in calming a client and assuring that the interview can be brought to a safe conclusion: for example, telling a client about whom you are concerned that he can leave anytime if he begins to feel upset or uncomfortable; or, if he seems to you to be getting upset or uncomfortable as he talks about a particular subject, suggesting that he need not talk about that issue right now; or, if he refuses for any reason to speak or appears angry or frustrated, suggesting to him that you stop for now and that he think about coming back when he feels more like talking. Further, if a client indicates that he wants to end a session, or if he gets up and leaves a session at any time, with or without an indication, let him go. Then discuss the way to approach this kind of behavior with your supervisor before planning another meeting with this client.

All these recommendations are based on two crucial assumptions. The first is your understanding that—unless a *great* deal is known about any client *and* a team decision has been made that it is clinically indicated-using confrontational or verbally aggressive tactics in any interview with any client is both risky and disrespectful, particularly since it is *never* your job to be judge and jury, regardless of the circumstances under which you meet a client. The second is your understanding that-even when a great deal *is* known about a client—you will always conduct your own mental assessment based on the tools you would use in any interview. If that assessment or your feelings about the client's potential for violent behavior suggest that someone (including you) is at imminent risk, you will listen first and foremost to yourself and act accordingly.

Finally, it is important for you to think about and, when appropriate, discuss with your supervisor your own limits for tolerating fears of violence. In so doing, you will be better able to accept two fundamental realities about the nature of this work: first, that you are going to be frightened of clients from time to time no matter how well you prepare yourself; second, that with experience and time you will become better able to accept your own feelings and fears and still be confident that you know when and how to adequately safeguard your wellbeing.

nine

How to Determine Whether a Client Might Hurt Herself

Just as the last chapter explored the idea that we might sometimes ignore thoughts that *we* could be in danger, so we must start this chapter by addressing the powerful wish to avoid thinking that another human being might deliberately take *her own* life. Yet, as we all know, suicide—quite literally—happens every day.

Some of those people who die every day might be acquaintances or friends or even relatives of ours. They could also be acquaintances or friends or relatives of our clients—or they could *be* our clients. If we accept that unthinkable thought as within the realm of possibility, then where should we begin, as therapists, to think constructively about the idea that someone we are interested in, care about, and wish to help might one day feel so desperate or hopeless or rageful as to take or attempt to take her own life? How do we realistically assess how much we can do to prevent such a terrible outcome?

First we must accept a sad but utterly truthful fact: Any person who truly wants to end her life, other than a very young child or a completely incapacitated adult, will find a way to do so. You may wish to change that, you may try to change it, you may believe you have changed it, but you may fail. That is a fact.

Having accepted that reality, you should know that there is a great deal you *can* do and *should* do and will *learn* to do that can significantly alter a client's feeling that life is not worth living, or that no one cares if she lives or dies, or that she cannot solve the problems that are making her consider suicide as a solution. The purpose of this chapter is to help you recognize those sentiments in a client, face them with her, and protect her from them as much as is humanly possible.

This chapter will explore how to assess and respond to suicidal thoughts and actions in both adults and children. If this last idea—that children can have such sadness or hopelessness or anger or fear within them that they wish to die—makes thinking about suicide seem overwhelming, then perhaps some facts repeatedly documented by research *will* be helpful. Let us begin with children and move chronologically along the spectrum of suicide.

Deliberate suicides have occurred in children as young as four years old, but in general suicides under the age of 12 are uncommon.

Among adolescents, girls are considerably more likely to *attempt* suicide; however, boys are considerably more likely to *complete* a suicide.

The most frequent suicide *attempts* occur in *women under 30;* then the incidence of attempts begins to decrease. Also, women tend, in general, to use less reliably lethal methods of trying to kill themselves, such as overdoses of pills or slashing their wrists.

The most frequent *completed* suicides occur in *men over 45,* and the risk factor continues to grow—particularly in white males—culminating in the greatest rate of completion after age 65. In addition, men use more certain methods, such as guns, hanging themselves, and jumping from high places.

Those are the bare-bones statistics about the *populations* most at risk. It is hoped that these statistics—like all statistics—are reassuring because they are verifiable and relatively neutral. However, as a therapist you must also recognize and think about the powerful *myths* society has concerning suicide, two of which have been proven over and over again *not* to be true, but persist anyway, even among therapists—sometimes with fatal consequences.

The first myth is: *A person who is thinking about killing herself will never tell anyone.*

The *fact* is that *most* people who take their own lives have given some sign of their intentions to at least one other person—and often to several other people—within the last few weeks or months. That sign may be verbal and quite direct-whether said in a joking manner or quite seriously. For example, a person may say, "I wish I was dead," or "I think I may kill myself," or "What do you suppose it's like to be dead?" or some other clear statement indicating to those around her that she is having thoughts about ending her life.

Or it may be said less directly, for example: "I'm so tired I wish I could sleep for years," or "Nothing interests me anymore," or "What difference does it make if I failed that exam?" or many other variations that suggest despondency, or hopelessness, or a lack of interest in the future or in her own well-being. Or it may be expressed as anger and a wish for revenge against another person who has disappointed her, or threatened her feeling of being loved, or humiliated her, such as "I'll show him who can leave. . . ."

In addition, there are many nonverbal ways in which a person might indicate to others that she is thinking about hurting herself or that she is losing interest in staying alive. She might stop eating, or give away some possessions, or have her telephone disconnected, or start taking drugs, or go to a doctor for a physical symptom.

Finally, the most dramatic and significant way in which a person might indicate that she is thinking about suicide is by making an attempt on her life that is not fatal or even necessarily very dangerous in and of itself. The purpose might be to see how others respond or to "practice" not caring what happens to herself. In either case, a suicide attempt should certainly be regarded as a foreboding sign.

These are some of the common ways by which to recognize that the first myth about suicide—that most people who are going to kill themselves do so without any warning—is simply not true. It is hoped that this clarification will go some way toward reassuring you that if a client of yours is thinking about killing herself there is a very good likelihood that you can get some indication, provided you know when and how to ask and are able to both listen and talk about suicide yourself.

This brings us to the second myth about suicide: *If you talk about suicide, that will put the idea into a person's head and she will kill herself.*

The facts are that *talking about suicide does not cause suicide* and that *not* talking about suicide with someone who is thinking of hurting herself can sometimes be a fatal mistake. Nevertheless, most of us need some help in knowing what to say, what to ask that might be helpful, and how and when to bring up the subject. So let us start with the last question: how and when you would consider raising the subject of whether or not a client you are seeing, especially for the first time, might be considering suicide.

Again, you would begin with the existing record on that client, starting first with the *diagnosis* and looking up the criteria. As in the case of violent tendencies, you are looking in both children and adults for diagnoses that include impulsivity, poor judgment, antisocial or suicidal tendencies as part of the criteria for the diagnosis itself. If there are no indications of any of these, then you would next be alert to any diagnoses that suggest depression or intense anxiety. However, as with all diagnoses, the absence of such criteria is never in and of itself a reason to rule out the possibility that a client might be thinking about or even planning to hurt herself.

Next turn to the *mental status exam*, paying particular attention to the previous questioner's comments on the client's suicidal ideation at that time. This lets you know if the client has told someone before that she was thinking about hurting herself. In addition, be alert to the person's predominant mood at the time the MSE was formulated and to any thoughts that were preoccupying her at that time, so that you can assess, as you do *your* mental status exam, whether or not this person continues

---

REMEMBER

- Talking to a client about her suicidal thoughts makes it *less* likely that she will kill herself.

to be "stuck" on the same unhappy or unrealistic thoughts she was having then. Further, note any history of delusions, depersonalization, or hallucinations—especially command hallucinations ordering her to hurt herself or someone else.

Focus next on her written history, looking for three essential elements. First, ascertain whether the client is a *substance abuser*, because, as was mentioned in the previous chapter, alcohol and drugs engender behavior that people might not otherwise do. That is, they are "disinhibitors" which both physiologically and psychologically limit the user's capacity to think logically, to move steadily, and sometimes to appropriately protect others and herself. Drugs, alcohol, or both have been implicated in at least half the known suicides in the United States; they figure even more prominently in adolescent suicides.

In addition, read the written record for any *family history of suicide* or suicide attempts. Is suicide seen in this client's family as a means of problem-solving? Has suicide ever been used as a way of relieving medical or psychiatric suffering? Whatever the reason, any previous suicide in your client's family places her at higher risk for suicide.

The last critical factor for which you would examine the record is *a history of previous suicide attempts by the client*, since the single most reliable predictor of a suicide attempt in the future is a suicide attempt in the past. If that suicide attempt has occurred within the last year, the client is in the highest risk group for another, possibly fatal attempt.

If you saw such a profile in the written record of a client, you might feel that you did not even wish to see her. That is certainly an issue you should discuss with your supervisor, because it is important and useful for you to explore your own personal experiences related to the issue of suicide and to think ahead about your feelings concerning such a client, just as you would before any first interview.

However, it is also important for you to realize that people who come for help are people who have problems, many of which they have not yet found a way either to resolve or to tolerate. What that means in practical terms is that at some time in your career you are certainly going to have a client who has made a suicide attempt—whether that information appears in the written record or not. And just as certainly, you are going to find it necessary at some juncture to evaluate a man, woman, or child for the possibility that one of them is presently thinking about, or planning, to kill him or herself.

So the first thing you need to do for yourself is to get comfortable with the idea that you are going to be talking to people from time to time about suicidal thoughts and behavior. You are going to find out what procedures exist in your agency for managing potentially suicidal clients. For example, who are you to speak to if such a scenario occurs? What telephone number do you call? Where do you ask a person to wait if you need to consult with a colleague? What have other people on the staff done in such situations?

Next you are going to explore in detail what your legal obligations are. For example, if someone reports to you that she is seriously thinking about or has a plan to kill herself, what rules of confidentiality, if any, apply? Who must you notify, and when? What kinds of notes do you need to keep during the session? What kinds of forms do you need to fill out after the interview? To what agencies and governing bodies are you required to report such a discussion? What follow-up, if any, is necessary?

In other words, you are going to get as much practical information as you can, because practical information is extremely helpful in overcoming the tendency to deny that someone you are with might be having thoughts or fantasies about hurting herself. When you are actually face-to-face with a client, regardless of what has been said or what you know about that person, if you have the *slightest inkling* that she might be suicidal, you must rely on that inkling enough to slowly but surely explore with the client whether or not she has had, or is presently having, any thoughts about killing herself.

The operative words here are "slowly but surely." That is,

REMEMBER

- **You must find out what your legal obligations are if a client tells you she is thinking about killing herself.**

you are going to ask questions in a deliberate and calm manner, reminding yourself at such times of two crucial facts: first, that people who are having thoughts of killing themselves are both relieved and grateful to have someone else bring it up; and second, that many people *think* about killing themselves from time to time but most of them neither wish to die nor actually take their own lives.

So where do you begin if you are having some feeling of unease about this client? The answer is: with a broad question, such as, "How are you feeling?" or "How are things these days?" What you are listening for in the answer is despair, despondency, or hopelessness. For example, as you explore a little with the client, does she express any feeling that things in her life are unbearable? Or that she feels unable to go on? Or that she is so lonely for someone who used to be in her life but is no longer that she cannot imagine the future without that person?

These kinds of feelings are more easily articulated by adults than children. If you are interviewing a child, particularly under the age of nine or ten, you will need to help her describe how she is feeling and the seriousness of the feelings she is experiencing. Therefore, when you are trying to assess the possibility of suicidal thoughts or feelings of despair in a child, always give her something by which to measure them. For example: "Do you think you feel more happy or more sad today?" "When you are sad, are you so sad you cry?" "Do you cry in the day and the night?" "Do you cry when you are alone, or when there are other people around?" Use a similar technique for angry feelings, or feelings of missing someone important who has died or gone away recently, or feelings that she has done something wrong.

Once you have begun to get a sense of the broad parameters of the client's mood, you want to find out if, when she is feeling that badly, she ever has any thoughts about hurting herself. Obviously, the answer you are wishing and hoping for is "Never," or "Are you kidding?" or "I'd be too scared to do something like that," or "I could never do that to my children," or just plain "No." However, as much as you might wish for one of those answers, eventually someone is going to say "Yes," and no matter how many times you have practiced such a scenario in your head or talked about it with your colleagues, you are still going to feel frightened.

At first, you will be tempted—despite all your preparations—to try and talk the client out of having those thoughts, rather than exploring them with her. You may find yourself wanting to say, "You shouldn't be thinking about things like that," or "Don't be silly, you have so much to be grateful for," or some other variation on these themes. The younger the client, the more likely you are to feel the temptation. But you are going to have to resist it.

What will help you to do so is to again remind yourself that lots of people *think* about killing themselves at one time or another. Also remind yourself that, because the client has acknowledged having such thoughts, you now have a mandate to explore them with her and to rule out the possibility that she might go beyond just thinking about suicide. Therefore, regardless of when this subject comes up in an interview, and regardless of what else you might have on your calendar to do after this interview, you should make a practice—both for the client's well-being and your own—of never letting a client leave your office until you have used all necessary resources to satisfy yourself that she is not at imminent risk of trying to kill herself.

Let us return to the moment at which you inquire about whether or not a client ever has thoughts of hurting herself and the answer is "yes." In clinical parlance, this is what constitutes *suicidal ideation*. When you uncover the presence of suicidal ideation, two things are required of you: First, if you are not already doing so, you must start taking notes, as carefully as possible. Second, once you have established the existence of some form of suicidal ideation, you need to know what the *content* of that ideation is. So you are going to ask the client some

---

REMEMBER

- **Most people who are thinking about killing themselves don't really want to do it.**

question like, "When you think about hurting yourself, how do you imagine doing it?" The response you get to this question will be somewhere on a spectrum between, "I don't know, I never really get that far," to "I think about jumping off the roof of my building," or some other comment that suggests thoughts of a specific mode of suicide.

Or you may first get a response from the client like, "I'm not really gonna kill myself," or "I was just kidding," or some other reaction intended to change the topic of conversation or minimize the seriousness of this very serious subject. At this point, or whenever it seems most appropriate, let the client know that you are glad to hear that she isn't really going to kill herself, because you don't want anything to happen to her.

This is a very powerful message, and its purpose is twofold. It is a reassurance to a person of any age that someone else is concerned about her and that—were she, in truth, actually giving serious thought to taking her own life—someone else cares whether or not she does so. Second, it demonstrates that you take everything she thinks and feels very seriously, particularly any thoughts she might have about killing herself; therefore, you are going to need to ask a few more questions to make absolutely certain that she is safe.

You next want to find out *when* the client last had a thought about hurting herself. Obviously, a response such as "this morning" is more significant than "two years ago when I broke up with my boyfriend." In either case, however, pursue information about *how frequently* those thoughts occur or occurred. For example, if the answer was "this morning," then you would want to know whether the client had these thoughts yesterday, and if so, how many times. And if she had them yesterday, you want to know when she started having these thoughts and whether they are happening more or less frequently than before. Also, when she is having these thoughts, are they fleeting? Or do they seem to be coming with greater *intensity* and interfering more with her life?

When you have ascertained those impressions from her, you need to find out *how comfortable* the client is with those thoughts when she does have them. For example, you might ask her how she feels when she has those thoughts. The response you are hoping for is one that suggests that they "scare the hell out of me" or "they really upset me." However, if there is any suggestion in the client's response that these thoughts are soothing or seem like a solution to all her problems, or promise reunion with a loved one, then that would significantly affect your evaluation of the state of imminent risk to this client unless the client is a child.

Very young children are the most significant exception. Children under the age of seven or eight may *appear* to be comfortable with the idea of dying because they probably don't know in any real sense what it means to be dead. Therefore, if a child says that she wants to be dead so she can see her grandfather, you need to find out whether she thinks she could talk with her grandfather if she were dead. Could she go out and play? Or bring her grandfather back home with her? If the child demonstrates a clear understanding that death is a real ending of her life, that all the bodily functions cease, and that the separation from her caretakers is real, then you must believe that her wish to die is quite serious.

Once you have explored how clearly the client understands the idea of dying, and how comfortable that idea seems to her, turn your attention to whether or not the client has ever tried to kill herself. If she has, how did she do it? While she is explaining that attempt to you, ask yourself: Was this last attempt not completed because the client's own better judgment or wish to live intervened? Or would this person be dead now were it not for ignorance on her part of what actually constituted a fatal dosage, or someone showing up unexpectedly, or some other piece of sheer luck?

At this point—or perhaps even earlier, depending on what the client has already told you—you may have decided that you are going to need a second opinion on whether or not this client is in imminent danger. Once you have begun to think that is necessary, the question then becomes: Why would you continue to explore this subject with the client, rather than leaving that to someone with more expertise or experience?

The reasons are twofold. First, once a client has begun to share such information with you and to feel your concern, she may be more willing to go into details or share her plans with you than with someone else. In fact, in a subsequent interview, she might deny that she has any thoughts of hurting herself.

Therefore, the more specific, detailed information you can share with the other interviewer, or team of people, the more likely it is that the client will get the level of care she needs to guarantee her safety.

Second, depending on the setting in which you work and the severity of the client's danger to herself, getting that level of care may entail having your supervisor join you and the client, or arranging for the client to be interviewed by your staff psychiatrist right then, or contacting your local emergency room and taking the client there, or waiting with the client until a member of her family is available to come and get her. However, it might also require that you call the police to take the client to a hospital or that you present your findings to a team of psychiatrists who will use that information as part of their deliberations on whether or not to hospitalize a client involuntarily. So the thoroughness of your interview not only is good practice but may also be crucial to protecting the client's safety—and her rights.

Very often, though, clinicians feel uneasy—particularly in those settings where they are the client's primary therapist about pursuing an interview when they realize that the client is telling them information that will need to go outside the confines of the confidential relationship between the two of them. Somehow, it begins to feel sneaky, or underhanded, or manipulative to ask further questions when you know you cannot keep the answers to yourself.

SIX THINGS YOU NEED TO FIND OUT IF
A CLIENT TELLS YOU SHE IS THINKING
ABOUT KILLING HERSELF

1. **When did she last have a thought about killing herself?**
2. **How often does she think about killing herself?**
3. **How comforting do these thoughts seem to her?**
4. **Has she made a previous suicide attempt?**
5. **Does she now have a plan to kill herself?**
6. **Can she carry out the plan?**

Should you reach this juncture with a client who is describing thoughts of killing herself, two ideas are useful. First, anyone willing to tell you her feelings, or thoughts, or plans to kill herself is almost certainly doing so because she wants you to help her not to. Second, if that is not the case, and she truly does want to harm herself, then a human life is at stake and you must certainly act to protect her.

Having ascertained a history of her previous attempt or attempts, turn your attention to whether or not this client presently has *a plan* to kill herself. If she had previously indicated some thought such as, "I'd jump off the roof of my building," return to that comment and explore it further. For example, ask her if she has actually gone up on the roof recently or, if the client is a child, whether she can actually get to the roof on her own.

If she has made no previous comment suggesting a plan, then ask some simple, straightforward questions such as, "How would you do it if you were going to kill yourself?" Again, you are hoping for the vaguest possible response suggesting the least premeditation. But if the client says, "I would take a bunch of pills," or "I would shoot myself," or "I would jump out a window," then you need to proceed in a very deliberate manner to evaluate the issue of *access to means*, which will, in turn, help you to determine the *level of premeditation*. For example, if a person says, "I would take a bunch of pills," ask what kind of pills she would take. She may say, "I have no idea," or "I don't know, maybe a bunch of aspirin"; both of those answers are quite different from saying, "I got a bottle of uppers put away," or "When my mother died, I kept everything she had in her medicine cabinet."

Clearly, the latter two responses suggest that this person has been thinking about the possibility of ending her life for some time. The same would be true of someone who has access to someone else's gun, such as a child or adolescent who reports that her father has a gun in the top drawer, or to an adult who tells you she has recently purchased a weapon.

With all clients but especially with children, listen for and explore the temptation to some more impulsive, although somewhat premeditated, form of suicide. For example, if a child tells you she would jump out a window, find out if she knows *what* window she would jump out of. If she says, "the one on the stairs at school," find out if she ever has gone near that window when it was open, whether or not there is ever a time when she can go near that window without being seen, and whether or not she has ever actually climbed out on the sill.

Obviously, by this time you will have reached a conclusion about whether or not this person might do something danger-ous to herself and made a decision that someone else needs to be informed. However, before you raise that subject, there is one more piece of information you want to garner, particularly with a child. That is *why* she wants to kill herself at this time, although you are not going to phrase it that way. Instead, you are going to ask the person something about what she thinks will happen if she tries to commit suicide. If you don't already know, you may hear an answer that will help illuminate for you what current conflict is making the client feel so desperate. For example, "My mommy will feel sorry she hit me yesterday," or "I won't really die, I'll just scare everybody," or "I won't have to worry about my ex-husband's bills," or "My boyfriend will be sorry he dumped me and we'll get back together again," or "My sister will come home and find me."

Whatever the answer, respond to it by telling the client, in one way or another, that there are many other solutions to the problem that is making her feel so badly at the moment, but that your first concern is making sure that she doesn't hurt herself. Especially if this is a new experience, you should always err on the side of caution if you have any doubts about the need for a second opinion.

You should have discussed well in advance with other mem-bers of the treatment team what the procedure is in your agency; this is the time to implement it. Once you have done all that, you should feel a great sense of relief and of accomplishment.

However, regrettably, it is not always that simple to assess whether or not a client might hurt herself, since those who have the most serious plans or are the most depressed or without hope are often the least communicative. You have to fall back on your own inklings or sense that the client is withdrawn, or angry, or threatening, or despairing to the point where it is not even worth talking about. Or you may be alerted by exactly the opposite phenomenon. That is, feelings of serenity or good humor in a person who has only recently been very depressed and whose present state of tranquility may indicate that she has finally made a decision to end her life. In all these cases you will seek a second opinion—even if your suspicions are based only on a disquieting hunch.

When you have done all this, you will have used all your resources, insight, and courage to raise the possibility with your client that she might be thinking of taking, or preparing to take her own life. But you must be realistic about your own limitations. If a client wishes to die, she will find a way to do so, despite your best efforts.

Ultimately, she is the person responsible for preserving—or taking—her own life.

This form begins with questions you should ask yourself in *every* interview. If the answer to some of these is "yes," then you should follow up with the client to find out whether or not the client has any suicidal ideation or intentions.

Questions for yourself

1. Is the client in a group that is statistically at high risk for suicide?
2. Has the client unintentionally gained or lost more than 5% of her body weight in the last month?
3. Has the client reported any marked change in sleeping habits?
4. Does the client appear sad or withdrawn?
5. Does the client sound despondent?
6. Has anyone else reported that the client is despondent or sounding hopeless?
7. Does the client seem extremely angry or hostile?
8. Does the client report a sudden improvement in mood or lifting of a longstanding depression?
9. Has the client recently experienced the loss of a significant person in her life through death, divorce, removal, or abandonment?
10. Has the client reported any recent suicide among friends or family?
11. Has the client reported any history of suicide in the family?
12. If so, does the client's family talk about the suicide or is it a secret?
13. Is the client approaching the anniversary of a family member's suicide?
14. Is the client about to be the same age or in similar circumstances as the family member who killed him/herself?
15. Has the client reported to you a previous suicide attempt?
16. Has the client made any comments—joking or otherwise—suggesting that death would be preferable to life?
17. Has anyone else reported that the client talked about killing herself?
18. Has anyone found a note, poem, or printed literature involving death or suicide that was written by or belongs to the client?
19. Does the client report giving away possessions?
20. Does the client have a history of impulsivity, poor judgment, or antisocial behavior?
21. Does the client have a history of recurrent depression, intense anxiety, or panic attacks?
22. Does the client have a history of a serious mental disorder, especially auditory hallucinations commanding her to hurt herself?
23. Does the client have a history of substance abuse?
24. Is the client frequently involved in "death-defying" or high-risk behavior?
25. Does the client frequently pick fights with people who are much larger or more dangerous?
26. Is there a current crisis in the client's life, such as illness, job loss, divorce, school failure, or suspension?

(continued)

Questions to ask the client

The list begins with general questions designed to establish whether or not a client is having suicidal ideation. You may or may not need to use these questions to establish the existence of that ideation; however, once ideation is reported, you should pursue the subsequent information in as much detail as possible.

1. You seem upset. Just how badly *are* you feeling?
2. When you feel badly, do you ever have any thoughts about hurting yourself?
3. Do you ever wish you were dead?
4. When you wish you were dead, do you ever think about killing yourself?

If the answer to these questions is yes:

5. When did you start having these thoughts?
6. What was happening when you started thinking about hurting yourself?
7. How often are you having these thoughts?
8. Are you able to stop these thoughts once you start having them?
9. When you think about killing yourself, do you think a *lot* about it?
10. Do these thoughts upset you or do they make you feel better?
11. What do you think would happen if you tried to kill yourself?
12. Who do you think would try to prevent your suicide?
13. Have you told anyone that you're thinking of killing yourself?
14. What do you imagine death would be like?
15. When you have thoughts of killing yourself, how do you imagine doing it?
16. When you imagine it, do you complete the suicide? If not, who or what stops you?
17. Do you imagine writing a suicide note? Have you actually written a suicide note?
18. Where do you expect to get the [gun, pills, knife, etc.] with which to kill yourself?
19. When you feel this way, do you talk to anyone about it?
20. Is that person a comfort?
21. Is there anyone who is so important to you that that person could keep you from hurting yourself?

ten

How to Determine Whether a Client Is a Substance Abuser

There are very few subjects in the field of mental health about which you will find more controversy than the issue of substance abuse. A discussion of the reasons why people resort to dangerous or illegal drugs, or why they drink, or why they abuse medications given for some other purpose will often produce as many answers as there are participants.

Some will say substance abuse is a disease with identifiable genetic or chemical or neurological indicators, and its sufferers should be regarded no differently from anyone else who is suffering from a chronic, debilitating illness. Others will point to social ills like poverty and racism as significant causal factors in the use of substances to remediate the painful realities of a harsh and innately unfair life. Still others will tell you that drug use is a moral flaw that hurts society and—as with other antisocial behaviors—its perpetrators should be left to the wisdom of the judicial system.

Even the definition of a substance abuser is murky. Diagnostic manuals make a distinction between use, abuse, and dependence. Social observers of one stripe or another describe the sorry state of a society filled with crackheads and drunks while they define themselves as "social drinkers" or their children as "smoking an occasional joint." Even those who openly acknowledge buying and selling and using substances they know to be both illicit and physiologically harmful will not hesitate to reassure you—and themselves—that they and their customers do so only "recreationally."

Were it possible to agree upon a concise definition of what constitutes substance abuse, it would still be close to impossible to get a consensus on how to respond therapeutically once you have identified an abuser. One end of the spectrum is represented by those who believe that the best person to help an abuser recover is another recovering abuser—hence the various "twelve-step" programs. Others advocate for individual treatment with a professional trained especially to work with substance abusers. Still others suggest that group therapy is the only effective modality, or that any well-trained therapist should be able to work with a substance abuser.

Different approaches also prevail as to what aspect of help must come first. For example, yours may be an agency where the belief is that, regardless of the problem with which the client presents himself, if he is deemed to also have a drinking or drug problem, that must be the initial focus of treatment, even if that means a brief hospitalization, or "detox" program. Or the substance abuse might be viewed in your clinic as just another self-destructive symptom of an underlying problem that must be addressed before the abuser can give up his substance.

By now it should be clear that consensus is unlikely on any aspect of the issues involving substance abuse—except one: There is little doubt in anyone's mind that the use and misuse of alcohol and drugs play a significant role in other destructive and self-destructive behaviors. They affect job performance and marital relationships, disease statistics and crime statistics. Homicide, suicide, and physical abuse of both adults and children are all correlated with substance abuse in more cases than not. And since substance abuse does seem to be a precipitator of other dangerous behaviors, every clinician must learn to think about, and then assess for, possible substance abuse.

One reason to do so is because this may be the key to *preventing* some of those other dangerous or destructive behaviors. For example, as you develop a profile of the circumstances under which battering or sexual abuse occur, you may be more alert when a client describes his alcohol or drug use pattern—to the need to carefully monitor the home situation, or to help the potential perpetrator to change some behavior, or, if he feels he cannot change, to teach him to remove himself temporarily from the setting when he feels he might act impulsively.

So where do you begin your assessment for possible substance abuse? You can start by looking at the other behaviors in which the client is involved. Examples of that were discussed in Chapters Eight and Nine, where part of your assessment involved consideration of whether the client's wish to die or to hurt someone else was being exacerbated by drugs or alcohol.

Beyond those two circumstances, the rest of this chapter will be devoted to helping you understand the *general areas of assessment* you are going to use in evaluating whether or not a client is a substance abuser. At the end of this chapter you will find more specific questions to ask of yourself and the client if any of the information you have garnered in the general areas caused you to be concerned. Of course, you will then share those findings with the treatment team in order to decide how next to intervene.

However, before we begin, it is important to add one additional factor to the equation of assessing for substance abuse. That is, substance abusers often do not want other people to know about their habit. They may feel ashamed, or know they are involved in illicit behavior that could lead to their arrest, or be denying to themselves the seriousness of their use—or any of a dozen other reasons for not bringing the subject up in an interview.

Therefore, if you don't ask, the issue may never get raised. Unfortunately, even if you do ask—and even if you have some information that makes you reasonably certain that a person is a user—he may still deny it when you bring it up. Or, if he does tell you, he may minimize the problem. Consequently, understanding the degree to which this person misuses some substance will not be easy. You will have to learn to ask about many different aspects of the problem in order to get a reasonably accurate picture of the degree to which drugs or alcohol play a part in-and interfere with—this client's functioning.

This last idea—that what you are ultimately trying to ascertain is what part drugs or alcohol play in a person's mental, physical, social and professional life—is what assessment for substance abuse really consists of. So begin by raising the topic in the context of one of the routine areas of your assessment. For example, if you are taking a brief medical history, you might ask the client if he smokes, and then if he drinks, and then whether or not he has ever used any drugs. When talking about his family history, you would certainly want to follow up with the client if he indicates that any other family member has a substance abuse problem.

The first general area to explore is *what substances* the client uses. Does he drink beer? Does he smoke marijuana and drink beer? Does he smoke cigarettes and marijuana and drink beer but "never touch hard liquor"? Does he ever use cocaine or heroin or valium, etc? That "etc." is an important one, because it is shorthand for a very long list of legal and illegal substances that can be misused, including some common over-the-counter medications. In your efforts to inform yourself about substance abuse, you should use whatever resources are available to familiarize yourself with the wide variety of substances that might be imbibed, injected, smoked, sniffed, or swallowed.

Once the client has acknowledged some substance use, explore *how long* he used or has been using that substance or substances. For example, an alcohol abuser can probably tell you the first time he ever took a drink. And a heroin user can almost certainly tell you the first time he ever shot up, and who gave him the heroin. This fact, in and of itself, is an interesting and significant one in your assessment—that is, that, especially with alcohol, the first time the substance was encountered seems to stand out in the mind of an abuser.

However, those reminiscences will not necessarily lead to an acknowledgment on the client's part that he is currently a user. So you would next turn to the question of *how recently* the substance or substances were used. Obviously, the answer, "I've been going to AA for 20 years," has different implications from "I don't remember" or "Maybe last week" or "This morning."

This last response raises an interesting dilemma for a clinician, and one which you should clarify with your supervisor. Especially if you have had limited experience in assessing for symptoms of substance abuse, you may discover during a session that the client is presently under the influence of drugs or alcohol or both.

In such a scenario, the client is probably not so intoxicated as to be apparently drunk or high. Even if he were, there is some disagreement in the therapeutic community as to how to handle such a situation. Some say that you should stop the interview at that point and suggest that the client come back when he is sober or not acutely experiencing the effects of the drug, since he is not likely to be able to make good use of the session under the circumstances. Still others recommend that you try and discuss with the client what effect he imagines the intoxication might have on the usefulness of therapy. Then there are those who would suggest that you simply continue the interview and explore, as much as possible, the history of the substance abuse. In any case, talk with your supervisor about what the agency deems an appropriate response and what services you can refer the client to if he is not suitable for your program.

Presuming that you are going to continue your assessment, the next area to focus on is *how much* of the substance the client uses. As you will see from the questions at the end of the chapter, you are trying to get a sense of the quantity of alcohol consumed, or the amount of marijuana smoked in a 24-hour period, or the number of pills taken and their dosage. However, the purpose of these questions is not for you to then be able to determine with certainty whether or not the client has a drinking or drug problem, because, unfortunately, making such a determination is not that simple.

Alcohol and drug use have very different meanings in different cultures within our society; in fact, depending on your own cultural and social background, you may feel frightened by or judgmental about behavior that is outside the context of your own experience of drugs or alcohol. For example, you may feel intensely concerned about an inner-city youngster for whom experimentation with whatever is being sold on his local street corner is considered a rite of passage, or with an employee who works the night shift and tells you that everyone at his job drinks beer from the time the boss leaves until the day shift starts. Your concern may be well-founded—or it may not—which is why a thorough assessment, as well as the input of the treatment team is necessary.

Listen, especially as you move into assessing the quantity of the substance used, for two things: First, does the client seem to have used the same quantity of the substance consistently for a long period of time or does he continue to increase the amount? If so, by how much has it increased and in what period of time? Second, if he is increasing the amount-regardless of whether his friends consider it a rite of passage, or everyone else on his job drinks, or whatever other social or cultural attitudes may prevail—does the client himself express any belief or concern or question about the possibility that he already has or is developing a drinking or drug problem?

This question may come up at any point during the interview. If it does, then—as with all other issues that the client experiences as sources of concern—you are getting an indication that he wants some help. However, if he does not bring up any worries about it at this point, then continue with the next general area of questioning, which is: *When does he use?*

Here you are listening for an elaboration of the circumstances, or times of day, or company in which the client drinks, takes drugs, or medicates himself. It would be reassuring at this point if we could say that a particular pattern indicates with certainty that the client is having a problem. However, regrettably, the nature of the different substances varies, and so does the nature of the definition of a problem.

In fact, the person who drinks a half bottle of wine for dinner by himself every night and has done so for twenty years may be at less risk than the person who is getting drunk every other

---

ASK YOURSELF

- **What substances does the client use?**
- **How recently has he used them?**
- **How much does he use?**
- **When does he use?**
- **Why does he use?**
- **What happens when he uses?**
- **What effect is the substance use having on his life?**
- **Has he ever tried to stop using? How did he try? Did it work?**

weekend with his friends. Just as the person who uses cocaine every three months at a party may be at less risk than the person who routinely "rolls a couple of joints" for himself as he is driving home from work. Part of the problem—even in citing such examples—is that they arouse social values and judgments which can imply approval or disapproval of the behavior. It is crucial that you remind yourself that your task is to gather information, so that later you can evaluate all the data and make a useful decision.

Implicit in the last question—when he uses—is the potential answer to the next question: *Why does he use?* This is not a question you will ask directly, and the possible answers are legion. Does he use because it makes him feel more comfortable in crowds? Does it ease his chronic physical pain so he can continue to do his job? Does it enable him to perform better sexually? Do all his friends do it? Does he do it to avoid thinking about the fact that he is going to be demoted? Or go bankrupt? Or lose his children? You may hear many explanations as you explore this area, but you should not feel surprised if you find no clear, concise answer.

However, as you move onto the next question, the client may be more helpful. That question is: *What happens when he uses?* Here you are listening for, and asking about, behavioral or personality changes. For example, does he have blackouts and forget how he got home? Or is he more at ease at parties? Is this when he hits his children or spouse? Does he become more daring in his transactions at work? Does he begin to hear voices or feel like things are crawling on his skin? Does he feel euphoric and believe, for that period of time, that all his troubles are behind him?

If the latter is the case, what are the troubles to which he is referring, and are they being caused by the substances he is using? In other words: *What effect is his substance use having on his life?* For example, is his spouse threatening to leave him because of his substance use? Has he been arrested for drunk driving, or selling drugs, or embezzling funds he used to pay for a drug habit? Does he tend to socialize only with other users? Are his current physical problems related to his substance use? Is he about to get fired from his job because he doesn't come to work on time, or is unreliable, or doesn't perform his job as well as he used to?

By now you can no doubt see that there are many steps in assessing whether or not a client might need treatment for a substance abuse problem. It is likely, by this point in an interview, that if the client has been willing to answer your questions, he too recognizes that his substance use is having quite a serious effect on his life. Regardless of whether or not he acknowledges that fact, there are three more questions to explore, if possible, before you present your findings to the treatment team. These are: *Has the client ever tried to stop using? If so, how did he try?* And lastly, *Did it work?*

When you have the answers to these questions, you will have finished your assessment of the client's history of substance abuse. This assessment should prove invaluable in helping the treatment team to carefully calibrate the level of intervention necessary for this particular client.

ASSESSMENT FOR SUBSTANCE ABUSE POTENTIAL

It is unlikely that you will ask a client all these questions. However, since it is common these days to find multiple substance use and abuse, you will need to tailor your choice of questions to reflect information derived from the first six responses.

1. Do you—or did you ever—smoke cigarettes? For how long? How many per day?
2. Do you drink?
3. What do you drink? (Beer, wine, liquor?)
4. Do you take any prescription medications regularly? How do they make you feel?
5. Do you use any over-the-counter medications regularly? How do they make you feel?
6. Have you ever used any illegal drug?
7. When was the last time you had a drink/used?
8. How much did you have to drink/use?
9. When was the last time before that?
10. How much did you have?
11. Do you always drink/use approximately the same amount? If not, is the amount increasing or decreasing?
12. (If it is increasing) does that concern you?
13. Have you ever gained or lost a significant amount of weight when you were drinking/using?
14. Have you ever had difficulty sleeping when you were drinking/using?
15. At what time of day do you drink/use?
16. At what time of the week do you drink/use?
17. How many days a week do you drink/use?
18. Who is usually with you when you drink/use?
19. Do most of your friends drink/use?
20. Do (or did) your parents drink/use?
21. Is there anyone in your family who is an alcoholic/addict?
22. Have you ever been concerned that you might have a drinking/drug problem?
23. Has anyone else ever suggested to you that you have (or had) a drinking/drug problem?
24. How does drinking/using help you?
25. When you drink/use, how does it make you feel?
26. Do people ever report behavior to you which you don't remember doing while you were under the influence of alcohol or drugs?
27. Do other people report that you become more careless, or angry, or out of control when you've been drinking/using?
28. Are you able to "handle" more alcohol or drugs than you used to be?
29. Are you less able to "handle" alcohol or drugs than you used to be?
30. Do you feel more sociable when you've been drinking/using?
31. Have you ever had sex with someone with whom you would not have had sex if you weren't drinking/using?
32. Do you ever feel regret about any behavior after you've been drinking/using?
33. Do you drink/use to "get away from your troubles"?

(continued)

34. What troubles are you trying to get away from?
35. Has anyone at your job expressed concern about your drinking/using?
36. Are you aware of any way in which drinking/using is interfering with your work?
37. Have you missed any days at work because of drinking/using?
38. Have you ever lost a job because of drinking/using?
39. Are you having any difficulties or conflict with your spouse or partner because of drinking/using?
40. Has your spouse or partner ever threatened to leave you if you didn't stop drinking/using?
41. Has a spouse or partner ever left you because of your drinking/using?
42. Does drinking or drug use ever interfere with your sexual relationships?
43. Have you ever been arrested for the use or sale of drugs or alcohol or because of your behavior when under the influence?
44. Do you pay less attention to your family because you are drinking/using?
45. Do you avoid your family or friends when you have been drinking/using?
46. Have you ever hit your spouse or children when you've been drinking/using?
47. Are you having financial difficulties?
48. Are they related in any way to your drinking/using?
49. Have you ever tried to stop drinking/using? How?
50. Have you ever seen or heard things that weren't there when you were drinking/using?
51. Have you ever had any form of therapy to help you stop drinking/using?
52. Have you ever attended a twelve-step or other support group to help you stop drinking/using?
53. Have you ever been to a doctor to stop drinking/using?
54. Have you ever been hospitalized for drinking/using? Where? For how long?

eleven

How to Assess Chldren for Neglect, Abuse, and Sexual Abuse

Of all the situations that provoke sadness, fear, or anger in a clinician, none is as intense as an adult's hurting or degrading or molesting a child or leaving the child so unprotected that she becomes prey to someone else doing those things. Neglect, abuse, and sexual abuse can be unbearably painful to think about. However, even as we are wishing, hoping, and praying that such things never happen to another child, the law, and society, and our own consciences demand that we think about them, learn to recognize the *possibility* that they might be occurring and, when we have reason to be concerned, inform others about that concern.

It is especially important to think about and understand the meaning of the word emphasized in the paragraph above: that is, the *possibility* that neglect, abuse, or sexual abuse is taking place. Unless you work in an agency whose mandate is to make a determination about whether such behavior is occurring, your responsibility as a clinician is to raise your concerns with the appropriate person or agency and to provide all relevant documentation -*not* to *prove* that a child is being neglected, abused, or sexually abused.

Every state has its own law defining abuse and neglect, and every state has a system for reporting them. They also have their own designations of *who is required* to report. These designations may be based on professional training, licensure, job description, etc. Therefore, your first task is to clarify whether or not you are a *mandated reporter* of suspected child abuse. If you are a mandated reporter, that means there can be legal consequences for you if you *do not* report suspected abuse or neglect.

Whether you are a mandated reporter or not, your agency will undoubtedly have guidelines concerning the need to report suspected abuse and neglect. Your second task is to familiarize yourself with those guidelines and to talk with your supervisor about how they are implemented. Ask to see the forms which must be filled out and find out to what agency in your state such reports are made.

It is especially important in cases of suspected abuse or neglect that you do everything you possibly can to *avoid making a unilateral decision to report*. You should use the support and experience of those around you to guide you and to calm the inevitable anxieties that are raised by having to talk with parents or contact a child welfare agency. The obligation to inform another agency also carries with it a particularly powerful responsibility to be conscientious and deliberate in your information-gathering, since both a child's safety and the well-being of a family may be at risk.

The first purpose of this chapter therefore, is to help you make that conscientious and deliberate assessment so that you have garnered as much data as possible for your consultations with more experienced staff members. The second purpose is to provide both the tools and the confidence so that, should you find yourself in a situation where you believe that a child is at risk and you *truly* have no one else to advise you, you will act without hesitation to protect that child's safety.

The chapter will clarify the concepts of neglect and abuse

REMEMBER

- **Find out if you are a mandated reporter of child abuse and neglect.**

How to avoid making a
unilateral decision to report
child abuse or neglect

1. Learn your agency's procedures regarding suspected abuse or neglect.

2. If possible, only schedule first interviews with children when a senior staff member is at your agency.

3. If # 2 is not possible, see if a rotation of senior workers on call by telephone might be possible.

4. If # 3 is not possible, ask for your supervisor's home telephone number and for clarification of the circumstances under which you should use it.

5. Ask for your agency director's home telephone number and for clarification of the circumstances under which you should use it.

6. When you think a child's safety is at risk, do not let feelings of embarrassment or feelings that you "shouldn't bother her at home" stand in the way of calling a senior staff member, your supervisor, or the director of your agency.

---

and discuss some of the ways in which they might become evident in a session. You will learn what to ask if such information does arise and how to assess the imminent risk to the child. In addition, this chapter addresses the three critical areas to think about routinely when seeing a child in order to evaluate the risk that this child is being either neglected or physically/sexually abused. These three areas are: *physical symptoms*, *behavioral signs*, and *caretaker characteristics*.

You will find a detailed list of physical symptoms, behavioral signs and caretaker characteristics at the end of the chapter. The reason for this list is not just to provide you with an easy reference but also to remind you that there are many clues to the possibility that a child is being hurt, some of which may not in and of themselves seem related to abuse or neglect. Therefore, it is important to familiarize yourself with the possible *combinations* of signs, symptoms, and caretaker characteristics which could be indicators as well. The list is also intended to help you avoid jumping to conclusions. Especially when you are feeling anxious, you must resist the tendency to rush rather than soliciting all the information needed to make a conscientious decision.

So, keeping all those aspects in mind, let us first begin with a preliminary demarcation between neglect and abuse, bearing in mind, however, that definitions and language also vary from state to state. What is described here as neglect may be referred to in your laws as maltreatment or abuse; physical abuse may be called excessive corporal punishment. Broadly speaking, however, *neglect* can be defined as the parent or legally designated caretaker *not doing something for the child* that should have been done, whereas *abuse* can be conceptualized as the parent or legally designated caretaker *doing something to the child* that should not have been done.

It is perhaps confusing to note that both of these definitions involve action or inaction only by the parent or legally designated caretaker, since it is certainly true that someone other than a parent or caretaker might hurt a child and that you might become aware of such an incident and correctly assess that you have a responsibility to inform the appropriate agency.

For example, a man might physically or sexually abuse his girlfriend's child. Depending on the laws in your state and the nature of his action against the child, his behavior might be deemed by the courts to be assault, rape, sodomy, or some other charge. On the other hand, the mother who for whatever reason left her child unprotected from harm might be deemed neglectful because, as stated above, neglect implies the *absence* of some action that the parent should have taken, and it invariably arises out of inertia or a lack of something in caring for a child.

This lack manifests itself in five different identifiable forms of neglect, the first and seemingly most apparent of which is *physical neglect*. The operative word here (as it is with all five types of neglect) is *seemingly*, because trying to assess whether or not a situation is potentially neglectful can sometimes bring into play significant cultural and social differences, which can cloud one's judgment in making a sound assessment. For example, if an infant was brought to your office who was dirty, or dressed in ragged or seasonally inappropriate clothing, or was unwashed, you might be repelled, angry, or convinced she was neglected. However, if the child were 12, her appearance might have a different meaning—just as it might if the family were newly arrived from a very different culture, or homeless, or of a particular religious persuasion, or refugees, or even just returned from a camping trip.

Therefore, in your assessment of any type of prospective neglect, it is important to ask yourself two questions: First, is the condition in which you find the child one which appears to have been going on *over a period of time?* In other words, do you have some information to suggest that this is the typical level of caretaking this child receives? Second, might it be *endangering the health or safety* of the child? If the answer is yes to either question, then you can feel more confident that what you are observing, hearing about, or feeling anxious about requires further evaluation.

Let us now return to the definition of physical neglect, since it involves more than assessing a child's appearance. Broadly speaking, physical neglect not only refers to inappropriate or insufficient clothing but can also be used to describe a situation involving inadequate shelter, sanitation, or food. Given the parameters described above—that is, length of time and risk to the child's health or safety—it should not be terribly difficult to know if the child's well-being is at risk.

If you feel concerned but aren't sure, then ask—not in an accusatory or inquisitorial way but in a way that transmits your concern both for the parent's wish to be a good parent and for the child's well-being. Ask the child or ask the parent, depending on which seems most appropriate and likely to give you the clearest sense of what is happening to the child. Ask when the child last ate, or had a bath, or had clean clothes. Ask where she lives and how many people live with her. Ask if she has a room. If not, ask if she has a bed, and if she does, how many people sleep in it. Ask what she had for breakfast, or who fed her. And, if the answers seem crucial, write them down.

The second kind of neglect about which you must be concerned is often directly related to the first-that is *medical neglect.* The most straightforward example of this would be a child who is not getting enough to eat and is suffering from malnutrition, but there are many other examples as well, for instance: giving a child some dangerously inappropriate medication or remedy for a condition or illness; or not taking her for regular medical follow-up of a potentially serious condition; or any other absence of the provision of medical treatment without which the child might die or lose some essential bodily function.

The third area of concern is *educational neglect,* which means, quite simply, that the child is not going to school or being educated by some acceptable alternative system for reasons having to do with the need or condition of the caretaker, not of the child. For example, an alcoholic or depressed parent may be up all night and sleep during the day, making it impossible for the child to be brought to school on any consistent basis. Or a parent may routinely keep an older child at home as caretaker for a preschooler or an ill sibling.

Fourth is the neglect arising out of *inadequate supervision.* This refers to leaving a child alone or untended at an inappropriate age; exposing a child to dangerous circumstances, such as a surrogate caretaker who is mentally or physically unfit to protect the child; placing a child in situations where she may see or hear or participate in activities that are unsuitable, such as pornography or prostitution or the use of drugs; or simply the abandoning of a child.

Lastly, there is *emotional neglect,* in which a parent scapegoats a child, isolates the child from human contact for long periods of time, or humiliates the child. In addition, a parent might constantly threaten the child with dire consequences, subject her to some other form of mental duress, or just ignore her for long periods of time.

Those are the five ways that neglect can manifest itself and some examples of each. As you have no doubt realized by now, potentially neglectful situations can sometimes be precipitated by events over which the caretaker may have very little control. That reality poses a particularly thorny problem for the clinician.

In fact, homelessness, substance abuse, a death in the family, a job loss, mental illness or retardation, or many other circumstances may explain why a child is not being cared for properly. And all those extenuating circumstances may contribute to feelings of guilt and confusion on your part about whether or not

you have the right to add to this parent's burden by raising issues about a child's well-being. This is one of the reasons why
it is especially important for you to share the information you
have with your supervisor and the treatment team *as early as
possible*, so that you will have their guidance in deciding what
you must do to protect the child.

This is, of course, equally true in cases of possible *physical abuse*, which can be defined as an *intentional* rather than
accidental causing of injury to a child. These injuries may include bruises, burns or bites, beatings, stabbings, broken limbs,
or many other forms of physical injury. The injury itself may be
apparent when you see a child, or it may be hidden. It may have
been the result of one incident or an ongoing series of assaults.
It may have happened yesterday or last month or last year.

You are going to have to tailor your inquiry about possible
abuse according to many factors. For example, one child may
be of an age where she can easily describe what has happened;
another child's experience may emerge only as she plays with
dolls or does a drawing. One child may tell you she is "accident prone," while another explains that she always wears long
sleeves on Mondays because she stays at her father's house on
the weekends.

And every child will have a very different understanding of
the implications of what is happening to her. One might readily
volunteer information about injuries and why, how, and under
what circumstances her parent or parents punish her. Another
might tell you what happened but just as quickly explain that
it happened because she was bad, or didn't listen, or ate too
much popcorn. Others may be suspicious, or guarded, or make
up incongruous explanations for marks or bruises that you can
see, or deny that they have any marks on their body that can't
be seen, or simply become visibly frightened, silent, or tearful.

Just as you must learn to appreciate the myriad ways in
which children will inform you that they are being physically
abused, so, too, there is a wide range of knowledge and opinion
among parents of what constitutes abusive behavior toward a
child. These views can vary enormously according to cultural
and ethnic values in the community. For example, what may appear to be excessive physical punishment of a child may be seen
by the parent, as well as many in the subculture of that parent, as

appropriate discipline, without which the child would become unruly or disrespectful. And that parent may be completely unaware that such discipline might constitute child abuse in the broader culture.

At the other end of that spectrum are parents who are very much aware of what the law considers abusive behavior, or who have warned their child to lie about marks or injuries or suffer further punishment, and who know how and where on a child's body to inflict injury where it is least likely to be observed. In addition, parents may have had previous reports of suspected child abuse made against them; they may even have had this or some other child removed from the family after a previous finding of abuse by an agency designated to protect children.

Given this wide range of understanding on the part of parents of the meaning of their actions and your understanding of your responsibility to protect a child, you must use common sense while you are conducting an interview. Ask yourself how you can best acquire the information you need to be certain the child is safe, while making certain you are not doing anything that might further endanger a child about whom you may already have concerns.

Common sense and tact are equally necessary when assessing a child for possible *sexual abuse*, which, simply defined, refers to any use of a child for a sexual purpose. That purpose can range from fondling to oral, anal, or genital intercourse. It may have occurred once or many times. It can be perpetrated by a man or a woman. It can be perpetrated against a male child or a female child. The child can be 15 days old or 15 months old or 15 years old.

Regardless of the nature of the sexual interaction, the age of the child, the gender of the perpetrator, or the number of times the abuse took place, there are two essential facts about sexual abuse of children to keep in mind: First, sexual abuse of children occurs in every race, ethnic group, and economic class in society. In other words, *anyone* can sexually abuse a child. Second, the perpetrator is most likely to be someone the child knows-either a family member or a friend who is trusted enough to have access to the child.

Depending partly on a child's age and partly on the manner in which the perpetrator has involved the child in the abuse (that is, threateningly or seductively), the child may reveal the fact that she is being sexually abused in various ways. For example, a young child may say something quite straightforward, like "Uncle Bobby put his pee-pee in me and it hurt," or play with two dolls in an overtly sexualized way and, when asked what the dolls are doing, simply tell you that they are "doing the thing like my babysitter does to me."

However, it is more likely, especially as children who are being sexually abused get older and the implication of what is happening to them become clearer, that they will experience shame and intense fear: fear of humiliation if the abuse is revealed; fear of being injured or killed; fear that they will be accused of betraying a loved one; fear of hurting a parent whom they believe is unaware of the abuse; fear of destroying the family. From the clinician's point of view the sum of all those fears is that in most cases it is extremely painful, even terrifying, for a child to reveal that she is being sexually abused.

All of the reasons to "keep the secret" can powerfully conspire against your asking the child—but you have to learn to ask anyway. If a child seems to know a lot more about sexual matters than makes sense for a child her age, then you need to ask in some simple, straightforward way, in language she can understand, where she learned all about that. If a child tells you that she doesn't like the way her babysitter touches her, then ask her to show you with two dolls how her babysitter touches her, or to point to the places on her body where the babysitter touches her. If an adolescent tells you that her mother's boyfriend is weird or her mother ought to get rid of the creep, you can ask what he says or does that makes her uncomfortable.

There are many ways to ask and, as you can see from the list at the end of the chapter, many indications of when it might be prudent to do so. So the question then becomes: If you ask a child about sexual abuse—or physical abuse—and she indicates that it is occurring, what do you do next?

The answer is that you try, without putting words in the child's mouth, to get some basic data, and you write it down. What is the *name* of the person who touched her or hurt her? Does that person *live* with the child? Is that person *at home* right now? *When* did, or does, the abuse occur? (For example, at night, or when mommy is at work.) *Where* did the abuse take

How to Report Suspected Abuse
or Neglect

1. Read over your notes from the session and underline or extract the material you need to report.

2. Some states have special telephone numbers to be used by mandated reporters. Make sure you call the right number.

3. Identify yourself by name and, if you are a mandated reporter, say so.

4. Identify your agency by name, address and telephone number.

5. Be prepared to give the following facts, if possible:

   (a) the child's name, age and date of birth

   (b) the parents' names

   (c) the names and ages of other children living in the household

   (d) the name of anyone else living in the household

   (e) the address and telephone number where the child who is the alleged victim lives

   (f) the parents' telephone numbers at work

   (g) the name of the alleged perpetrator

   (h) the alleged perpetrator's relationship to the child

   (i) the time and date when the alleged incident(s) occurred.

   (j) the place at which the alleged incident(s) occurred

   (k) a description of the alleged incident(s) as the child described them: e.g., the child reported that her father hit her approximately 10 times with an extension cord on the backs of her legs and on her face.

   (1) a description of any corroborating information: e.g., the child had seven thin red welts on the back of her knees and two marks on her right cheek.

   (m) some description, if the child told you, of what precipitated the incident: e.g., the child got a poor report card.

6. Ask the person who is taking the report for his/her name.

7. Ask for the number which is being assigned to the report.

place? (For example, in my cousin's bed, or at my big sister's house.) *What* did the person hurt the child with? (For example, his fist, his mouth, an iron, a belt.) *How many times/* has the abuse taken place? What was the *most recent occurrence*, including the date and approximate time of day, if the child can tell you? *Where on the child's body* was she hurt or touched? (The child can point to the places on her body and/or show you what she did to protect herself.) Does the child have any *marks or places that hurt right now?* And lastly, *whom* has the child told?

When you have that information, and while the child is still with you, inform your supervisor or some other member of the treatment team, so that the two of you can evaluate the information the child has given you. Based on that information, you and your supervisor together will do an *imminent risk assessment* before making a decision as to what to do next. That assessment will consist of evaluating a number of factors:

1. The recentness and nature of the abuse.
2. The age of the child and, therefore, the degree of dependency on an adult for protection.
3. The ease of access the alleged perpetrator has to the child.
4. The need of the child for immediate medical care or evaluation.
5. The capacity and reliability of the person who is responsible for protecting the child.
6. Any known previous history of abuse or neglect of this or some other child in the family.

Based on your joint evaluation of these factors, a decision will then be made as to how best to proceed in order to protect this child, including making a report to a child protection agency if that is necessary. When that is completed, next make sure you have met whatever obligations your agency has for documenting such an event and fulfill any tasks you are required by law to perform. When you have done all those things, you should feel reassured and satisfied that you have done everything *you* can to ensure that the child is safe.

PHYSICAL SIGNS OF NEGLECT

- Physical signs of neglect are observable. A child may look:
- Dirty or dressed inappropriately
- Listless or tired
- In need of dental care, glasses, or medical treatment
- As if development, including speech, is delayed

BEHAVIORAL SYMPTOMS OF NEGLECT

- A child may report that she:
- Is hungry
- Steals food for herself or other children
- Has never been to school or skips school
- Has no one to care for her at home
- Cannot stay awake

MOST FREQUENT CHARACTERISTICS OF NEGLECTFUL CARETAKERS

- The home is chaotic or disorganized.
- The caretaker is a substance abuser.
- The caretaker is socially isolated and lacks friends or family as sources of support.
- The caretaker demonstrates lack of interest or involvement in the child's hygiene, or safety, or emotional needs.
- The caretaker demonstrates a lack of interest or involvement in the child's medical needs.
- The caretaker exhibits a critical or demeaning attitude toward the child.
- The caretaker has a tendency to frighten or humiliate the child.
- The caretaker has a tendency to isolate the child from social or emotional nurturance.

SIGNS OF PHYSICAL ABUSE

Signs of physical abuse may not always be observable. They may be on parts of the child's body which are not readily seen. Pay particular attention to injuries that seem incongruent with the description of how the child got them.

- Burns, especially matching burns on both ankles or hands that suggest the child may have been immersed in hot liquid; cigarette burns; burns in the shape of objects, such as steam irons or curling irons.
- Bruises and welts, especially on both sides of the face or body, since accidental injuries rarely leave symmetrical marks; bruises that suggest that a child has been grabbed with two hands; patterned bruises which indicate the shape of an object such as a belt buckle, hairbrush or extension cord.

    (Bruises do not always look "black and blue." On darker skin they may look more like blotches, or shiny, or have a purplish cast. Bruises on lighter skin will appear purplish or yellow in successive stages of healing.)
- Bites
- Broken bones
- Injuries to the head or eyes

BEHAVIORAL SYMPTOMS OF PHYSICAL ABUSE

- The child is socially withdrawn.
- The child has frequent fights with other children.
- The child is unusually passive or compliant.
- The child exhibits concern or anxiety when other children get hurt.
- The child is fearful or guarded when her parents are present.
- The child is fearful or guarded around other adults.
- The child is fearful of going home.
- The child covers injuries with clothing or makeup.
- The child has repeated accidents.
- The child engages in self-mutilating or self-destructive behavior.
- The child runs away.
- The child makes a suicide attempt.
- There are reports from teachers of frequent crying or of learning difficulties in which an identifiable learning problem has been ruled out.

MOST FREQUENTCHARACTERISTICS OF
ABUSIVE CARETAKERS

- The caretaker perceives the child as being responsible for the caretaker's well-being.
- The caretaker has unreasonable expectations of the child's capacities.
- The caretaker uses forms of discipline which do not match the child's age or the child's behavior.
- The child is described consistently as "bad," "irresponsible," or "different" from other children.
- The caretaker is a substance abuser.
- The caretaker was abused as a child.
- The caretaker is socially isolated from friends, family, and community resources.

(continued)

- The caretaker sees him/herself as unable to "keep control."
- The caretaker is in crisis due to the loss of a loved one, possible incarceration, job loss, etc.
- The caretaker is mentally ill.

PHYSICAL SIGNS OF SEXUAL ABUSE

- Bed-wetting
- Indications or reports of pain, bruises, bleeding, or recurrent infections in the genitals or rectum, or recurrent urinary infections
- Indications or reports of pain, bruises, bleeding, or recurrent infections in the mouth
- Venereal disease in mouth, genitals, or rectum
- Sexually transmitted diseases in children who would not be expected to be sexually active
- Pre-teen or early teen pregnancy
- Recurrent vomiting or stomachaches

BEHAVIORAL SYMPTOMS OF SEXUAL ABUSE

- The child is hypervigilant.
- The child has sleep disturbances.
- The child reports fear of a particular person or place.
- The child is preoccupied with her own or other children's genitals.
- The child attempts sexual interactions with other children.
- The child is unusually mature, knowledgeable or seductive sexually.
- The child exhibits sudden social withdrawal.
- The child is fearful or unwilling to expose her body in normal situations (e.g., changing into a bathing-suit or during a routine medical examination).
- The child exhibits infantile behavior or excessive withdrawal into fantasy.
- The child reports having no friends.
- The child exhibits oversexualized or seductive behavior with a caretaker.
- The child becomes involved in antisocial behavior, e.g., truancy, delinquency, running away, substance abuse, prostitution, or other sexual promiscuity.
- The child engages in self-mutilating behavior or suicide attempts.

MOST FREQUENT CHARACTERISTICS OF
SEXUALLY ABUSIVE CARETAKERS

- All characteristics described as common in a family where physical abuse or neglect occurs would also apply in a family where a child is being sexually abused. In addition, the following characteristics are common.
- One caretaker who is passive and dependent, and one who is authoritarian
- A caretaker who is overly protective of a child
- A caretaker who is jealous of the child making an attachment to another person
- A caretaker who seems inappropriately seductive or who touches the child in what seem to be inappropriate ways

- One or both caretakers have experienced a history of physical or sexual abuse
- Marital or sexual conflict between caretakers
- Encouragement by a caretaker of the child's observing or participating in sexual acts with others, or in pornography or prostitution.
- A caretaker who is physically or mentally ill

twelve

WHAT PSYCHOLOGICAL TESTING IS AND WHEN YOU MIGHT ASK FOR IT

Throughout this book there have been frequent references to the treatment team, as well as recommendations that you make use of the other members as a resource for information, decisionmaking, validation, and reassurance as you proceed with your assessment. Depending on the nature of your workplace, the treatment team may or may not include a psychologist trained to administer psychological testing. Nevertheless, there may be situations when you and your supervisor decide that psychological testing might be helpful, and there certainly will be times when you will receive the results of psychological testing done in some other agency, such as a school or hospital.

If you have never before seen a psychological testing report, you may be completely bewildered by what you are reading. This chapter presents some basic information about the content and purpose of psychological testing, describes some circumstances under which you and your supervisor might consider that psychological testing be done as part of a client's assessment, and discusses how to talk to a client about the purpose of and process of psychological testing.

So let us begin with some basic facts about psychological testing.

First, although it may be administered for different reasons, psychological testing can be used for evaluating clients from preschool age to old age.

Second, psychological tests are useful, in part, because they are *standardized*. That is, although some of the tests are designed to assess children, and others are designed for adults, those that are designed for children are given in an identical fashion, with the same questions, and in the same order *to every child*. And those tests that are given to adults are given in exactly the same way to every adult. This means that an experienced psychologist interpreting the testing has the benefit of a body of preexisting data and experiential knowledge of how other children or adults have performed on exactly the same test, administered in exactly the same way.

Third, because the tests are standardized, the results offer the tester a view of the client which is based less on the client's ability or wish to present a certain impression of himself to others, and more on an assessment of the client's characteristic personality style, his thinking patterns, and his intellectual functioning. However, it is important to note that, particularly in this last aspect—intellectual functioning—there has been evidence that test scores can sometimes be disrupted by factors such as depression and anxiety, distractibility, and even by cultural bias in some of the tests themselves.

If you request psychological testing or receive such a report from some other agency, what is it likely to look like? First, unless it is a summary of the psychologist's findings, a report of psychological testing will usually start off by indicating the *name and age of the client, and the date or dates on which the testing occurred*. This may sound pro forma, but it is, in fact, important to note the dates of testing because certain tests cannot be considered reliable if they are repeated more often than every two years. The reason is that the client may give answers based on his *memory* of the previous testing, rather than because that is his characteristic level, or style, of response. If you are debating whether to test a client who has been tested in the past, this could be a factor in your decision-making.

Next, the report will generally give *a list of the tests that were administered* to the client. This will almost certainly include and usually begin with the current version of those tests intended to evaluate intellectual and cognitive functioning, such as the Stanford-Binet test or one of the Wechsler series. The latter includes the Wechsler Preschool and Primary Scale of Intelligence (WPPSI), for use with young children up to age six; the Wechsler Intelligence Scale for Children (WISC) for children up to age 16; and the Wechsler Adult Intelligence Scale (WAIS) for use with adults.

All three of the Wechsler tests have a series of subtests that evaluate intellectual and cognitive functioning in both verbal and nonverbal areas. These verbal and performance subtests are intended to measure ways in which different aspects of intelligence are demonstrated. How the results of these tests are described in the report will be discussed shortly.

Another series of tests that will often be listed are those which focus on the client's psychological and emotional functioning. This is typically accomplished in one of two ways: either by using standardized checklists that elucidate patterns of behavior through *observation* of the client; or by administering *projective tests*. Since the use of checklists to report behavioral observations is straightforward, we will focus here on how projective testing is used.

The most commonly used projective tests are the Rorschach and the Thematic Apperception Test (or TAT). The Rorschach is a series of symmetrical ink blots, some in black and white, some including colors. The TAT is a series of pictures of people in ambiguous situations that have some emotional content. These tests are referred to as projective tests because they present the client with a series of images or situations that could be seen as representing many different things or having many different meanings and it is left to the client to "project" his own personal meaning onto them.

The purpose of these tests is to get a sense of the client's inner world; that is accomplished by the tester asking the client to describe what he sees in the ink blots or, in the case of the TATs, to tell a story about what he thinks is happening in the picture. And since the ink blots and pictures are so vague, the client must draw on *his* experience of the world, his understanding of reality, his relationships with others, and his own unique hopes and dreams and disappointments.

However, it is important to note that, since the responses to the Rorschach and TAT vary more than those on the intelligence tests or the behavioral checklists, the interpretation of those responses is necessarily less standardized. Therefore, the experience and skill of the tester become more significant factors in the quality and reliability of the findings on projective tests.

Finally, there is often an additional group of tests listed which may have been administered in response to concerns raised in the original referral for testing, or because the psychologist routinely uses those tests and finds them helpful in the evaluation process, or because some questions raised by the intelligence tests required further exploration. There are too many such tests to list here, but their purpose can range from assessing developmental levels or nonverbal problem-solving skills to evaluating school achievement or identifying gross neurological problems.

Once the list of tests administered has been presented, the next section of the report will usually be *a brief description of why testing was indicated.* For example, it may say something such as: "Billy Doe was referred for testing by his teacher, at the request of his parent, because he is currently failing English and Science, and because his teachers report that he is inattentive or disruptive in his classes." Or, "Ms. Travers was referred for testing by her neurologist, Dr. John Smithers, because, following a fire in a chemical plant in which she worked and suffered smoke inhalation, Ms. Travers began to report fainting spells, difficulty in distinguishing left and right, and lapses of memory."

Following that description it is not unusual to find a brief history of the significant psychological events in the client's life and a brief narrative of his development and family background. This should be compared to your own findings, especially since your source of information about the client might not be the same person with whom the psychologist spoke. This is a useful way both to verify information you have about the client and to be alerted to discrepancies.

Next, the tester will usually devote a section to *observations about the client during the testing.* The purpose of this section is to present the tester's impressions of this client's behavior, his style of interacting, and his characteristic modes of problem-solving, involvement in tasks, frustration tolerance, and feelings of competence. Especially with a child, this description will help you to imagine how he behaves in other situations which require him to concentrate or work at a task.

Next, the report will focus on *test results*, usually beginning with the results of the Verbal Intelligence Quotient (I.Q.) subtest, then the Performance I.Q. subtest, and then a full-scale I.Q. score that puts the client's intellectual functioning into a framework compared with other children or adults of his age. For example, "Ms. Travers demonstrated a verbal I.Q. of 104, a Performance I.Q. of 105, and a full-scale I.Q. of 103."

Regardless of which I.Q. test is used (e.g., WISC, Stanford-Binet), levels of intellectual functioning are always indicated by a *range* of scores. Thus a full-scale I.Q. of 69 or below on the WAIS, WISC, or WPPSI is classified as mentally deficient; 70-79 is considered borderline intelligence; 80-89 is low average; 90-109 is average; 110-119 is high average; 120-129 is superior; and above 130 is very superior. Other intelligence tests may use other ranges, however, so it is important not to assume that all of them consider 100 to be the midpoint, or average I.Q., as the Wechsler tests do.

Following the full-scale I.Q. score, the tester will usually comment on the *numerical difference between the verbal and performance I.Q.s*, if there is one, and make a special note if those numbers are *more than 15 digits apart* (for example, a Verbal I.Q. of 117 and a Performance I.Q. of 98). If there is more than a 15-point differential and the client's full-scale I.Q. is in the average range or higher (that is 90 or above), then the tester is alerted to the possibility that the discrepancy indicates a *learning disability* which will require further evaluation.

The next section of the results will be devoted to a *description of significant findings* revealed by the testing. These findings might include an elaboration on the nature of the learning disability the tester suspects, or it might focus on some other

---

REMEMBER

- **Always ask the tester if she believes the report reflects your client's *true* capacities.**

aspect of learning style or cognitive functioning. Or it might describe the most salient aspects of the client's inner life and his perceptions of himself and the world. When a complete battery of tests is administered, it is likely that all these aspects of the client's functioning will be touched on. In addition, this section of the report should tell you whether or not the psychologist believes that these test results are an accurate reflection of this client's true capacities. If this information is not in the report, you should ask the tester that question if you possibly can.

Finally, there will be a section in which the psychologist makes *recommendations* based on her assessment of the client's functioning as revealed on these standardized tests. These recommendations can include anything from tutoring designed to remediate a specific learning problem to placing a client in a day psychiatric hospital where he can get more intensive services and observation than your facility can offer. They might suggest that a client pursue a particular career choice or be moved to a school setting better suited to his level of intellectual functioning. They might include a recommendation that the client be tested again after some course of therapy and/or medication to see if his depression has dissipated—or any of a myriad of other recommendations. However, whatever the psychologist's findings are, they all serve the same purpose: to provide an additional perspective on the client's functioning and potential.

Perhaps, though, you are having some doubts about how helpful psychological testing really is, especially since there has always been some lingering controversy about the validity of I.Q. tests in particular. And you might also be wondering about the effect that categorizing a person's intellectual functioning might have on the belief he or others around him have in his capacity to accomplish certain tasks. So why is it useful to find out such information, especially about a young child, whose test results regarding I.Q. are most susceptible to change over time?

Let us use a typical case example to illustrate how you and the treatment team might use the results of psychological testing to make a more informed decision about how—and perhaps even with whom—you could make the most helpful intervention. A mother brings her nine-year-old son for therapy because the school says he "needs help," reporting that the child is in a regular classroom setting where he is disruptive, is failing several subjects, and, according to teacher reports, is "not trying" and has become the "class clown." The parent, who speaks English but has some difficulty understanding it because it is not her native tongue, reports that she is frustrated and confused by the school's response and very disappointed in her child. She provides you with recent psychological testing results done at the child's school.

And let us say that you read that testing and it indicates that this child has been given the WISC and has demonstrated a full-scale I.Q. of 82, placing him at the low end of the low average range of intelligence. That finding would undoubtedly raise certain questions for you and your supervisor about the meaning of that child's behavior, the meaning of the mother's perception of the child, and even the meaning of the school's recommendation that he "needs help." If you discovered that this child had an I.Q. placing him in the average range of intelligence but with a significant enough difference between his verbal and performance I.Q.s to indicate the likelihood of a learning disability, you would have different questions. And still another approach would be indicated if the child had an I.Q. of 136.

So one of the reasons for psychological testing is to help you and your supervisor and the treatment team to arrive at appropriate interventions and a treatment plan that is based on a realistic and objective assessment of the client's intellectual functioning. And you might ask for psychological testing at an early stage in your assessment because you have some reason to think that there is a discrepancy between the expectations or perceived functioning of a client and his actual ability.

There are numerous other reasons why you might consider psychological testing, for instance, to document an improvement or a deterioration in a client's functioning since previous testing was done, or to further verify or identify a thought disorder, neurological impairment, memory problem, or learning disability. You might request testing to rule out the possibility that a client's inner life is impinging on his capacity to perform cognitively. Or the test results might be helpful in career counseling, or educational planning—even for determining the outcome of a legal proceeding such as a custody hearing or a case where a toxic substance or other agent has caused an assault on a client's neurological system.

However, all those good uses of testing notwithstanding, one must consider a caveat about introducing the idea of psychological testing at an early stage in your relationship with a client. Testing an adult takes a minimum of several hours. Testing a child may require a few hours each day for two or three days. It involves introducing another person into your relationship with the client in a significant role when your relationship is barely established. If the testing cannot be done at your facility, it may involve introducing another agency as well. Further, it may raise some additional concern on the client's part about what might be wrong with him. And, after all that, there is no guarantee that the results will provide you with any clear answers to the questions you have about this particular client *at this time*.

So, given those constraints on its usefulness as a source of information in the earliest stage of your assessment, as well as the potential for disrupting the relationship you are trying to forge, there are still times at which ruling out a learning disability or identifying specific strengths and weaknesses in various aspects of a client's functioning is either necessary or salutory to the therapy. Further, if you work in a school or a diagnostic evaluation center or another setting where psychological testing is a routine part of the information-gathering process, then one of your roles in the agency may be to prepare clients for testing.

So the question becomes: How do you prepare a client—especially a child—for psychological testing in a way that is not going to produce anxiety that could interfere with his test performance? You always start by explaining to the client—and to the parent if the client is a child—why you think the testing might be helpful. For example, "We know you're having difficulty in school but we aren't sure why. The test results will help us understand what you're having trouble with so we can figure out how to help you do better," or "We need more information about the kinds of memory loss you're having," or some other simple, straightforward explanation of why the testing may be useful.

Next, reassure the client-and again include the parent—that even though this is called "testing," it isn't a test like one has in school. That is, there might be one or two parts of the test that ask information questions, but there will also be puzzles, pictures to draw, and stories to tell.

Third, let the client know that these are tests where everybody gets some answers wrong, so he shouldn't be surprised when he reaches a point where he is having trouble answering the questions. The point here is that the tests are *designed* in such a way—particularly on the parts that have to do with fund of information—to become progressively more difficult, so that eventually the client will reach a level that reflects his capacity and will start getting more answers wrong than right. So you need to reassure the client that no one expects him to get all right answers and that he is not "failing the test" if he doesn't.

Lastly, if it is a child who is being tested, you need to give him some description of the person who will be testing him and where he will be going for the testing; if possible, show him the room where the testing will take place. You can also tell him that this person has tested lots of children you know. Answer any questions the parent or child might have about how long the testing might take, and how, when and by whom the findings will be explained to them. Then arrange an appointment with them for after the testing. You will use that session to talk about what the testing was like and to make sure the test results *were* explained. If they weren't, make arrangements for them to be. If they were, be certain that the client understood the explanation.

When you have done all that, you can feel certain that you have maximized the usefulness of the psychological testing for the client, yourself, and the treatment team.

thirteen

How to Write an Assessment

You have now finished your preliminary interviews and gathered all the necessary documents from other agencies to complete your assessment. What remains to be done is to write up your findings in some coherent useful way. The purposes of this chapter are to familiarize you with what is expected in an assessment, to offer some guidelines for the order in which information should appear, and to pose some questions to which you should provide the answers in writing your document. In addition, you will find a sample at the end of this chapter of a biopsychosocial assessment.

Before you begin to write, however, it is important to stop and think about who will be reading your assessment now and in the future. Further, you should ask yourself to what purposes this document, and the mental status exam which should accompany it in the record, might eventually be put. If you are a student or an intern, then the case might be transferred to another worker when you leave the agency, or perhaps *after* you leave the agency. That means another therapist in your agency will be relying on your assessment to provide information about the client. Under those circumstances, your assessment should be thought of as replacing a face-to-face discussion.

Beyond this obvious value of your assessment as an information tool for the next therapist, it may also be used at future treatment conferences, or some information from it might be given with the client's consent to a therapist with whom the client is considering therapy or to some other agency that can provide some services or care not provided by your agency.

Those are a few examples of situations in which your client might consent to the use of the assessment, or some part of it, for other purposes. There are also circumstances, however, under which your assessment might be used without your client's consent, or even without your consent. For instance, if the case has necessitated a report of suspected child abuse, then your assessment might become part of documents which the court subpoenas to evaluate the need for foster care or to decide who should get custody of the child. Under these circumstances, the content of your assessment and the care and accuracy with which you have written it could have long-term implications in the lives of other people. Obviously, it is important that you give serious thought beforehand to your use of language and to what you include in your assessment.

However, even *after* you have written your assessment and added it to the client's record, you must think about what is in it. For example, if you are writing about a client who has tested positive for HIV, then your state may require special protection of those records to ensure that the client is not subject to discrimination or to dissemination of that medical information except under very stringent guidelines.

Having given due consideration to all these aspects of writing an assessment, always start your document with the client's identifying data: name, date of birth, and the date on which you wrote or dictated the assessment. Your agency may prefer that you also put *your* name and title at the head of the assessment, or that you put it at the end of the document with your signature.

In either case, you next write one or two sentences which

ASK YOURSELF

- **Who else might read this assessment now and in the future?**

are an introduction to the client, again giving her name, a brief description of one or two salient characteristics, her age, her ethnicity, her religion, perhaps her grade and the school she attends, or her marital status. Following that is information which may be referred to as the "presenting problem" or the "current symptomatology." Whatever it is called, it should answer, in narrative form, two crucial questions:

- Who recommended treatment or made the referral?
- Why is the client in need of help at this time?

Following that, you next describe the household in which the client currently resides. This section should include answers to:

- Where does the client live?
- Who else lives there?
- Who takes care of whom?
- What work does each member of the household do?
- How does the family currently support itself?
- Is this a change in the family's financial or living conditions?

After that, most of the important historical and developmental information on your client should be stated in a chronological narrative, beginning, in the case of children, with information about their parents. For adults, it should begin with their significant recollections of their family of origin. Following is a list of questions to consider, beginning with those more applicable to adults. Depending on your client's age, some will be relevant and some will not. You should try to answer all those that seem especially pertinent to your client's history:

- Who constituted her family of origin?
- What was her place in the order of siblings?
- How does she characterize her relationship with her mother?
- How does she characterize her relationship with her father?

- How does she characterize her relationship with each of her siblings?
- How does she characterize her parents' relationship with each other?
- Which members of her family of origin have died?
- What contact does she have with surviving members of her family of origin?
- What were the significant emotional events of her childhood?
- How old was she when each of these events occurred?
- What effect did these events have on her?
- How was her health as a child?
- How was the health of other family members during her childhood?
- What was the family's involvement in the life of the community?
- What was the family's involvement in ethnic or cultural activities?
- What was the family's involvement in religious activities?
- Did she have a strong identification with a social, cultural, ethnic or religious group?
- Did she have friends?
- What schools did she attend?
- How did she do academically while in school?
- How did she do behaviorally while in school?
- What was the last grade in school that she completed?
- Why did she leave school?
- Did she ever serve in the military?
- What jobs has she held?
- For how long did she work at each?
- Does she currently work?
- At what age did she have her first sexual relationship?
- Has she ever been married?
- Is she currently married?
- If not, how did the marriage end?

- If so, what is the character of her relationship with her spouse?
- Has she ever been pregnant?
- Does she have children?
- What is the character of her relationship with her children?
- Does she have friends?
- Does she see them occasionally or frequently?
- Does she belong to any social, professional, cultural, educational, or religious organizations?
- Does she participate in their activities?
- Has she ever had any serious health problems?
- If so, what was the nature of the problems?
- Is she presently in good health?
- If not, what is the nature of the current health problem?
- Has she ever been in therapy before?
- If so, why did the previous therapy end?
- Has she ever been hospitalized for a psychiatric condition?
- Has she ever been medicated for a psychiatric condition?
- Has she ever had a problem with drugs or alcohol?

Obviously, some of these questions are not applicable to children or adolescents. If the client is a child or adolescent, you should include answers to the following questions:

- What were the medical, physical, social, and emotional conditions under which the child was born?
- How would you characterize the mother's relationship with the child?
- How would you characterize the father's relationship with the child?
- How would you characterize the child's relationship with her siblings?
- What have been the significant psychological events in the child's life?
- How old was the child when these events occurred?

- Did the child reach all developmental milestones within the normal time frame?
- If not, which milestones were early and which were delayed?
- Has the child had any significant health problems?
- If so, what were they?
- Is the child currently in good health?
- If not, what is the nature of the current health problems?
- Does the child have friends?
- How would you describe the character of these relationships?
- Does the child participate in any social, cultural, religious or educational activities?
- What school does the child attend?
- What grade is the child in?
- Is that the grade she should be in?
- If not, why not?
- How is the child doing in school at this time?
- Is that a change in school performance?
- What does the child's teacher report about the child's behavior and functioning at school?
- If the child has had psychological testing, what were the significant findings of that testing?

When you have completed the history, you next want to focus on describing the salient aspects of the client's treatment to this point. This section should include answers to the following:

- How many times has the client been seen by you for therapy?
- What is the current treatment modality?
- How frequently is the client seen for therapy?
- How does the client behave when she comes for therapy?
- How does the client behave toward you when she comes for therapy?

- Have the client's behavior or feelings changed since she started coming for therapy?
- If so, in what way?
- What do you see as the clinical issues which need to be addressed in therapy?
- Is the client motivated to participate in therapy?
- What are the client's goals in therapy?
- What is your estimate at this time of the client's prognosis?

The last item in a biopsychosocial assessment is a diagnosis. Ideally, this is arrived at in consultation with your supervisor and other members of the treatment team during a conference at which the modality, frequency, and goals of treatment are delineated. Arriving at a diagnosis is a complex process and one that has engendered controversy which it would not be useful to debate here. At this stage in your learning, however, it is important to begin familiarizing yourself with how to read a diagnostic manual, which diagnoses belong on which axis, and what the criteria are for some of the more frequently encountered diagnoses in your work setting.

Now all that remains to think about is how you are going to find time to sit down and actually write your assessment.

BIOPHYSICAL ASSESSMENT: A SAMPLE

Name: Mariana M.
Date of Birth: 2/26/85
Date of Assessment: 10/9/93

PRESENTING PROBLEM

Mariana M. is a petite, shy 8 1/2-year-old Catholic female whose mother is Panamanian and whose father was of Italian descent. Mariana was brought to the West City Mental Health Clinic by her paternal grandmother, Sofia P. Ms. P. was referred to West City by the Children's Protection Agency after Mariana was removed from her mother's home and placed in Sofia's temporary custody, following an incident in which Mariana was burned on her back with a steam iron six weeks ago. Mariana has repeatedly stated that she "fell on the iron," but medical findings and investigator's reports indicate that the burn could not have occurred accidentally. A hearing is set for next month to determine if Sofia will have permanent custody. Sofia reports that, since coming to live with her, Mariana has been refusing to do her school work, getting into fights with other children, stealing food at home, and lying to Sofia. She also reports some sleep disturbances and Mariana's "crying at the drop of a hat."

HOUSEHOLD DESCRIPTION

Mariana currently lives with her paternal grandmother, Sofia P., age 53, and her grandfather, Arturo P., age 58, both of whom are immigrants from Italy. Sofia works as a secretary in a law firm; Arturo is a tinsmith who works for an air conditioning company. They live in a two-bedroom apartment in the Ridgewood section of Fallston, where they have resided for 12 years.

HISTORICAL AND DEVELOPMENTAL DATA

Mariana was the result of a casual sexual liaison between Arturo and Sofia's only child, Paolo, and Carmelita A., a Panamanian whom Paolo met while stationed in Panama City with the U.S. Army. Paolo was 20, Carmelita was 21 and had a 2-year-old daughter, Alicia, by a previous liaison. While pregnant with Mariana, Carmelita followed Paolo to Fallston when he left the military. They had a conflictual relationship and did not live together.

Arturo and Sofia were unaware of Carmelita's presence in Fallston until three months later, when Paolo was hit and killed by a drunk driver. At his funeral, Carmelita told Arturo and Sofia that she was 5 months pregnant with Paolo's child, whom Carmelita stated she did not want. An agreement was reached that Arturo and Sofia would pay for Carmelita's prenatal care and would adopt the baby at birth. However, when Mariana was born, Carmelita changed her mind and, with financial assistance from Arturo and Sofia, brought Alicia from Panama and moved to a larger apartment with her two children.

Details of Carmelita's prenatal care prior to 5 months are unknown, but records from the Central Hospital Pre-Natal Care Clinic indicate that, when examined at 5 months, Carmelita suffered from anemia and asthma

(continued)

and was suspected of being a cocaine abuser, though she denied any substance use. She did not come for her appointment at 6 months and at 7 months had gained no weight since her previous visit.

Mariana was born 5¬Ω weeks early and weighed 4 lbs. 8 oz. Labor lasted 3 hours. Sofia states that she accompanied Carmelita to the hospital and that Carmelita was given no anesthetic during the delivery after a pelvic sonogram indicated signs of fetal distress. Mariana was born with the umbilicus wrapped around her neck. She was kept in an incubator for 5 days, after which Carmelita took her home for 3 days, then told Sofia to come and get her. Mariana remained with Sofia and Arturo for 4 months, during which time Sofia states that Mariana gained weight quickly, was a good eater, and slept through the night by 7 weeks.

After 4 months, Carmelita wanted Mariana back, but agreed she could spend every weekend with her grandparents. In addition, Sofia came twice weekly to the apartment to bring food and diapers for the children and to check on Mariana, whom Sofia reports "always seemed to pull into a shell at her mother's house." Sofia also took Mariana for all medical checkups and cared for her during routine childhood illnesses. Arturo and Sofia continued to request that Carmelita allow them to adopt Mariana.

This caretaking arrangement continued for the next 4¬Ω years, during which time Carmelita would occasionally disappear for several months at a time, leaving Mariana with her grandparents, who believe Carmelita was abusing drugs during these absences. Sofia weaned Mariana from the bottle at 16 months and toilet trained her at 2¬Ω years with no difficulty.

Just before Mariana's fifth birthday, Carmelita disappeared with her children for 8 months. Sofia has no knowledge of their whereabouts during this time but states that Mariana was "a different child" when she returned to Fallston, sometimes hoarding food in her bed when she visited Sofia on weekends and crying herself to sleep. When questioned by Sofia, Mariana "just looked terrified."

Carmelita told Sofia only that "Mariana went to kindergarten" during that period, but Sofia states that, when Mariana started first grade at Fallston Elementary School the next year, the teacher reported that "she has no idea what goes on in a school," and had probably never been to school before. Mariana quickly caught up to the other children academically, but isolated herself socially.

Since their return to Fallston almost 3 years ago, Carmelita has been involved with several men, two of whom have lived with her and her daughters in a one-bedroom apartment. She worked briefly as a mill worker, and then in a fast-food restaurant, and currently receives public assistance.

Sofia has been concerned on several occasions in the last year about bruises on Mariana, but Mariana has consistently stated that they were accidents and six months ago Carmelita warned Sofia that, if she did not stop asking Mariana questions, Sofia "will never see your grandchild again."

Prior to being burned, Mariana was attending the third grade at Fallston Elementary School. Reports from the school indicate that she received standardized state tests at the beginning of this year and was at or above grade level in all subjects. After Mariana was removed from her mother, Sofia sent her to St. Mary's, a parochial school in Webster. Her teacher currently reports Mariana is "unable to concentrate; frequently gets out of her seat; and, if she did know how to read before, appears to

(continued)

have forgotten it. She frequently initiates fights with other children, and has poor socialization skills."

Mariana has had no unusual medical history. She had recurrent ear infections as an infant, but has no evidence of any permanent medical problems as a result. She continues to be seen at Central Hospital Clinic for care of her burn, which her doctor reports is healing normally. In light of her mother's suspected substance abuse, she was recently tested for AIDS and the results were negative.

Mr. Daley, Mariana's caseworker at the Children's Protection Agency, anticipates that Carmelita will not attempt to regain custody of Mariana at the hearing next month. The Children's Protection Agency is continuing their investigation and will interview Mariana again next week. They are currently evaluating the need to remove Alicia from Carmelita's care.

CLIENT CONTACT

Mariana has been seen 1 time weekly for 4 individual sessions and twice with her grandmother. She is a vigilant, verbal little girl who is easily moved to tears. She states constantly that she misses her mother and is confused by the idea that her mother may not have treated her the way she should. She continues to deny that her mother burned her and says that her mother was "outside when I fell on the iron." She also states that she got burned "because I was bad." She has expressed a wish to come for therapy "every day" and seems to feel soothed by talking about these painful incidents, even though she continually states that she was removed from her mother, "because I didn't listen to her."

Mariana is able now to talk with some ease about her feelings, but, considering all the unknown aspects of her early experience and functioning, her prognosis at this time can only be approximated as fair to good.

DSM-III-R DIAGNOSIS

Axis I: 309.40	Adjustment disorder with mixed disturbance of emotions and conduct
Axis II: 799.90	Deferred
Axis III:	Healthy child with burn on back
Axis IV:	Psychosocial stressors: physical trauma and abrupt separation from parent
	Severity: 6-Extreme
Axis V:	Highest level of adaptive functioning past year: 4 - Fair

Prepared by Susan Lukas, MSW

fourteen

Where You Go From Here

Believe it or not, having read this whole book, added all these assessment tools to your array of clinical skills, and finished the writing of your first assessment, you have completed only the initial phase of treatment. It is hoped that, having gotten this far, you not only feel more assured but also have the will and capacity to move on to the subsequent stages. However, it is also hoped that you have realized that will and capacity are not sufficient to engage a client in therapy. Without concern, respect, and interested listening on your part, there will be no therapy. If you can remember that-and the importance of curiosity rather than criticism of that which is different from your ethnic, cultural, social, or emotional experience-you will not only love your work but also become a wonderful therapist.

This brief chapter will be devoted simply to pointing you in some directions you might go next in pursuit of that goal.

If you are currently in school, try to arrange your courses so you can learn the theory of family therapy or child treatment or whatever it is that you need to know at the same time as you are having the experience in your field placement. If that is not possible, and will not *be* possible, then ask someone who is in the course you wish you could take for a copy of the course bibliography.

For every subject that has been briefly covered in this book, whole volumes have been written on both theory and practice. They offer explorations of a wide variety of clinical, social, ethnic, cultural, ideological, and moral perspectives. Find what you need and read it. If you cannot find it in just one volume, go to the numerous journals for your profession. If they don't tell you everything you need to know, go to the journals of allied professional groups. In other words, seek and—given access to a halfway decent library—ye shall find.

Even if you are not currently in school, you can still continue to learn. In most cities there are societies, institutes, lecture series, and workshops, the purposes of which are to offer advanced training or opportunities for continuing education. If you live in an area where such opportunities are few and far between, you can initiate learning by contacting other clinicians in the region to participate in peer-group discussion or supervision. That is, you could meet regularly with others who have a similar interest in some aspect of clinical work to discuss theory or practice issues, always bearing in mind the importance of disguising material from specific cases.

In addition, whether you are a student or a full-time practitioner, you should make it a point to join at least one professional organization. Apart from their function as advocates for the interests of your professional group, these organizations usually publish a number of extremely useful documents: e.g., guidelines for ethical behavior and standards of practice; journals that reflect the current trends; a newsletter to keep you abreast of political concerns, practice management issues, and social activities; a membership list that provides you with names of peers in your area.

Beyond all these obvious benefits of belonging to professional organizations, they are also likely to be your most up-to-date resource for finding out your legal obligations as a therapist.

REMEMBER

- **Without concern, respect, and interested listening, there will be no therapy.**

Like all laws, those concerning our role and responsibilities are constantly being refined, changed, expanded, or overturned. New legislation or a court decision in one state may set a precedent that will eventually be adopted nationwide. What was appropriate practice yesterday may or may not be tomorrow. Even if you are a student today, being aware of these changes will ultimately become your responsibility, so it is probably wise to start learning about them now.

And that, ultimately, is the single most salient component of the work you have chosen; that is, continuous learning. It is both a demand of clinical work that you keep informing yourself in order to better understand and meet your client's needs and the pleasure and glory of the work. You will think, talk, read, teach, write, and dream about it—but it is unlikely that you will ever be bored by it.

INDEX

attributing own assumptions to a client,
16–17
client's attitude toward, 27
and the mental status exam, 15
comfort with clients' expectations, 89
danger to, 101–2
discussion of suicide with a client, 115
fear of violence, 111
feelings about a client's characteristics,
27
feelings about parents of a child client,
64
greeting a client, 5
information about confidentiality, 10–11
as an information-gatherer, 50
introduction of, to the client, 6–7
knowledge of child development, 58
need for information about medications,
40
observation versus inferences by, 67–68
preparation for an interview, 2–4
questioning a client about substance
abuse, 130–31
questioning of the potential of a client
for suicide, 126
relationship with the client, xvi
role in first interview with a child, 72
take-charge role in family interviews,
48–49
viewpoint of, and meaning of
observations in a mental status, 21
therapy:
alliance with parents in, 68, 75
for couples, 87–100
effect of intoxication on, 132
family, 44–57
family, reframing the problem in, 2
group, for substance abuse, 129
see also treatment
thought broadcasting, 23
thought process and content, client's, 20–25
and the mental status exam, 15, 29–30
time frame:
for assessing a client, the place of the
MSE, 14
and assessment of potential for violence,
105
of potentially neglectful behavior, 142
of substance abuse, 131
of suicidal thoughts, 120
for viewing a child's functioning, 79–80
timing:
of couples therapy, 91

of the presenting problem, 9
of therapy for children, 59
toys for children in an interview, 62
tranquility in a suicidal client, 125
treatment:
description in a written assessment,
167–68
individual, for substance abuse, 129
plan for, in a written assessment, 168
for substance abuse, 135
see also therapy
treatment team:
discussion about suicidal clients, 124
evaluation of a client's medications,
40–41
guidance from:
and cooperation in diagnosis, 168
in an imminent risk assessment, 148
in assessment of drug abuse, 132
in assessment of potential for violence,
104–5
in child neglect and abuse, 144
in refusal of a family for joint therapy,
57
and the limits of confidentiality, 10
psychologist as a member of, 153
reporting consultation with, to a client,
11
twelve-step programs, 129

understanding, asking a client for
clarification, 15

Verbal Intelligence Quotient (I.Q.), 157
verbal tests:
score versus performance I.Q. score,
157
Wechsler subtests, 155
violence:
preoccupation with, 104–5
and substance abuse, 129–30
threatened, in couple's therapy, 94
visual cues in a mental status exam, 17

Wechsler tests, 155
what, *see* questions/questioning
when, *see* time frame; timing
where, *see* questions/questioning; setting
who, clients included in a first interview, 3
why, see reasons
working alliance with parents, 68

xenophobia, 25